Responses to 101 Questions about Jesus

Michael L. Cook, S.J.

PAULIST PRESS
New York/Mahwah

Library of Congress Cataloging-in-Publication Data

Cook, Michael L., 1936–
    Responses to 101 questions about Jesus/Michael L. Cook.
        p.   cm.
    Includes bibliographical references.
    ISBN 0-8091-3428-4 (pbk.)
    1. Jesus Christ—Miscellanea.   I. Title.   II. Title: Responses to one hundred one questions about Jesus.
    BT295.C66   1993
    232—dc20   93-25492
                                                                              CIP

Published by Paulist Press
997 Macarthur Boulevard
Mahwah, N.J. 07430

Printed and bound in the United States of America

CONTENTS

FOR PAT AND DOROTHY,
   AND ALL THE "LITTLE ONES" WHO HAVE COME,
   AND ARE STILL TO COME . . .

INTRODUCTION

"But there are also many other things that Jesus did; if every one of them were written down, I suppose that the world itself could not contain the books that would be written" (Jn 21:25). Nor, one might add, the books about the books that have been written on the words and deeds, the death and resurrection, indeed the whole wondrous mystery that we simply refer to as "Jesus." So, why another book on Jesus? For me, the answer is both personal and professional, although I do not and cannot separate the two. I entered the Jesuits in 1953 at the tender age of seventeen, little aware of the person I was about to meet. I was attracted to the Jesuits by the ones I had come to know while attending Seattle Preparatory, but, as with many high school students of that time, God was for me a rather stern judge who would reward us if we were good and punish us if we were bad. Jesus was really just another name for God. That all changed when for the first time I encountered Jesus as a warm, human, personal friend while making the full thirty-day Spiritual Exercises of St. Ignatius Loyola. I met one who loved me, one who loved me fully for myself and who set no conditions to his love, but one whose love was powerfully transformative and freeing. I believe there is nothing more vital and central to a healthy spiritual life than the experience of being loved for oneself and the corresponding capacity to let that happen, to accept one's own lovableness as a free and undeserved gift. That was Jesus' gift to me.

But such love does call forth a response that includes taking responsibility throughout one's life. This takes place, of course, on many levels. For me, a central and decisive role has been that of professional theologian. I knew from that first very fresh and still

1

mysterious experience of the Spiritual Exercises that I wanted to
know Jesus more intimately, to love him more ardently, and to
follow him more faithfully. I knew even then that one path toward
the fulfillment of this prayer would be the study of Christology, i.e.
the study of who Jesus is and what we have said about him through
the centuries. I have been most fortunate to be able to do just that
over the course of some forty years as a Jesuit.

So, the first answer is that I am writing this book for myself in
the sense that it is an expression of love and gratitude to the one who
has loved me. Yet, as we know, the love of Christ impels us always
outward, to the love of others and especially of the "little ones" (Mk
10:14): children, widows, strangers, the poor and oppressed, and all
who seek God with justice, humility, and tenderness (Mic 6:8).
Hence, this book is written for all those people—students, friends
and family, colleagues, audiences of various sizes and shapes—who
have not just listened to me but have responded in ways that have
enriched and deepened this journey I have undertaken as a compan-
ion of Jesus. We are all "compañeros en Cristo" as St. Ignatius puts
it. Most of what I have written previously has been on a more scholarly level intended for the academy of professional colleagues. But
much of what I have experienced in classrooms, lecture halls, and
parish settings has been more pastoral and personal. I have long
been convinced that theologians, to be effective, must be involved in
some sort of pastoral work so that their professional, academic work
reflects the realities of the world in which we live, both the realities
of the average parishioner and the realities of those oppressed by
injustice. I have sought to be so involved over the years, and I hope
this book reflects the real questions of such people.

The present volume is part of a continuing series that began
with Raymond E. Brown's *Responses to 101 Questions on the Bible.*
It is written in the spirit of that book as "a people's book, not primarily a scholar's book." I have tried to formulate the questions as I
remember them coming from students, audiences, and friends. The
answers are intended as "responses" which come from my own understanding and approach. There are two things that should be
noted. Obviously, our primary source for whatever we say about
Jesus is the Bible. Hence, this volume assumes many of the questions about the Bible which Brown has already treated in his usual

incisive and admirable way. In addition, there will inevitably be some overlap with questions that Brown treats. I have sought to formulate and respond to them in my own way, but many of the questions are the same or similar. Also, while not ignoring my role as a theologian, my orientation is strongly biblical and my answers reflect that.

The second thing to note is that I approach this task with certain scholarly assumptions which should be mentioned at the outset. There are two images of Jesus that sometimes seem to be in conflict with one another. One is more traditional, the other more contemporary. Each image seeks to respond to the three most important questions about Jesus: who he was, what he taught, and what he hoped to accomplish. The traditional image, which has been the predominant one in the awareness of most Christians, places the emphasis on the "moment" of the incarnation. Jesus is the eternal Word of God who descended into flesh, died for our sins, and ascended back into eternal glory with the Father. This image is derived primarily from the gospel of John. "For God so loved the world that he gave his only Son, so that everyone who believes in him may not perish but may have eternal life" (Jn 3:16). What Jesus reveals or teaches is his own identity in his eternal relation to the Father, and what he hopes to accomplish is eternal life for all those who believe in him. He is the "way" who shows us the Father and so enables us to live within that same eternal relationship of Father and Son. The later creeds and councils of the church, which were influenced very much by John, placed such stress on the divinity of Jesus that the humanity has appeared to be absorbed into it. The orthodox fathers and councils always insisted upon the full humanity in principle. They maintained that if Jesus did not assume our full humanity, then we are not saved. But they frequently showed much less interest in the real, lived experience of the man Jesus from Nazareth. In their concern to maintain and defend the divinity of Jesus, they raised serious questions about how seriously they took the concrete manifestations of his humanness.

The contemporary image, on the other hand, is the result of the ongoing developments in biblical criticism, especially historical criticism, over roughly the last two centuries. One of the main results has been the recognition of the profoundly different character of the gospel of John in comparison with the synoptics, i.e. Mark, Matthew and Luke. For example, if one is asking a question about Jesus in his historical life and ministry—what he preached, what he hoped to accomplish, what he knew about his future or thought about himself—the synoptics will give us better access to that Jesus than the gospel of John or the subsequent tradition. This corresponds to a profound interest today in the human, historical man from Nazareth, the one who was like us in all things except sin (Heb 4:15). Many today want a Jesus who has walked with us on the way, who knows and understands because he has entered fully into the depths of human experience—the joys and the sorrows, the hopes and the fears, the struggles, trials, and temptations as well as the courageous efforts, the triumphs, the spiritual exultation that mark every one of us as human. This does not invalidate or deny the traditional image but it does qualify it. Jesus is not a God who only appears to be human. Rather, he is God's way of being human, the "human face of God," the one who became "obedient to the point of death—even death on a cross" (Phil 2:8). Obedience is a matter of human will, of the human struggle to remain faithful in the face of overwhelming suffering. The contemporary image does not deny the divinity of Jesus but it takes with the utmost seriousness the path that he had to follow in order to enter into the glory of the Father.

Another dimension of the contemporary approach that must be emphasized is that the New Testament writings as we have them are the end-product of a long historical process of interpretation and development. The stories about Jesus were first handed on by word of mouth, then written down and revised over a long period. The creeds and councils are part of this same process. Jesus comes to us today filtered through the varied and complex process of handing on what we call Christian tradition. We cannot simply equate what we say of him in faith with historical fact. The tradition about him contains much history but it also affirms many things, e.g. divinity, which are beyond the limits of historical methods as that discipline is understood today. The Pontifical Biblical Commission in 1964 and the Second Vatican Council in 1965 have affirmed with contemporary biblical scholarship that there are at least three stages in the gospel tradition about Jesus. There is *first* the period of Jesus the Galilean Jew who was born around 6–4 B.C.E. and died around 30

C.E. What we can say about his human, historical life depends on the validity of our methods of historical reconstruction—as does the next stage. So, *second,* there is the period of oral preaching by the earliest Christians from around 30 to 70 C.E. This occurs as the early Christians move out from the more rural, peasant village life of Jesus, whose principal language was Aramaic, to the urban life of Greek-speaking Jews and Gentiles. Although this stage is predominantly oral, Paul did begin writing his letters around 51 C.E., and some earlier, more primitive levels of gospel writing probably began about the same time or earlier. Finally, there is *third* the stage of the actual writing of the final edition of the canonical gospels as we have them. This begins with Mark around the time of the destruction of the temple in 70 C.E. and culminates with the final edition of John around 90–100 C.E. Clearly, the gospel authors in their final editions have incorporated many elements from the earlier stages of the tradition, ". . . selecting some things from the many which had been handed on either by word of mouth or in writing, reducing some of them to a synthesis, explicating . . . some things in view of the situation of their churches, and preserving the form of proclamation but always in such fashion that they recounted to us the honest truth about Jesus . . ." (Vatican II, *Dei Verbum* #19, tr. by J. Fitzmyer). The "honest truth about Jesus" includes history but is much more far-reaching. The biblical authors were theologians who interpreted the tradition about Jesus in the light of their own contemporary situation in order to proclaim his significance more effectively both within their communities and in their missionary outreach. We must do the same today if Jesus is to continue to be alive, active, and present in our midst. For we hand on not a dead letter from the past but a living Spirit.

Christology, which is my field, is just such an ongoing attempt to remain faithful to the past traditions about Jesus precisely by proclaiming him anew in the contemporary situation. The purpose is to continue to tell the story of Jesus, a story that never ends. We must continually reflect upon and interpret his story so that it transforms us and frees us, so that his story becomes our story as we follow him in discipleship. In striving to be true to the total tradition from the time of Jesus to the present, my approach to Christology includes four distinct but inseparable and indispensable dimensions: the historical Jesus, his death on the cross, the resurrection, and the incarnation. There are some today who would dismiss the incarnation as irrelevant and unnecessary for Christian faith. In my view, it is the most essential of all Christian faith-affirmations because it is the most radical. Incarnation affirms the personal self-involvement of God in our human history and our human experience. Nothing touches more deeply the very core of our humanness. God has become one of us. God has experienced from within what we experience, has suffered what we suffer, has remained faithful where we need to remain faithful. What could be more radical than that? But, in the light of contemporary approaches, the affirmation of incarnation is only possible as embracing the total experience of Jesus: his human and historical life and ministry, the central and decisive "event" of his death-resurrection, and the ongoing life and ministry of the church, beginning with Peter and Paul and John and continuing to John Paul II and beyond. I would agree with those theologians and biblical scholars today who would "recontextualize" the Johannine-patristic-conciliar tradition (the traditional image) within a more historical and processive or developmental view of Jesus (the contemporary image). To affirm that Jesus is the very incarnation of God is not possible without a critical analysis of the interpretive process that has brought us to such an affirmation. The affirmation of the Council of Chalcedon (451) that Jesus is fully human and fully divine within the unity of one person did not take place in a vacuum. The councils too were end-products of a long process of historical interpretation. This book will attempt to respond to some of the questions that arise out of our continual need to interpret and understand our tradition.

Finally, with regard to questions that people ask, an apparently simple and straightforward question can raise very complex issues. One such question which is frequently asked is: Did Jesus know he was God? For this or any other question, it is important to keep in mind what kind of question is being asked. Is it an *historical* question about what Jesus actually said and did during his life on earth? Is it a *psychological* question about his interior states of mind, i.e. what he was thinking about or intended to do, or the motives underlying his actions? Is it a *theological* question about the various ways that people have understood and interpreted his relationship to God over the centuries? Such theological interpretations might be found in the Bible or in church creeds and doctrines or in the works of theologians and biblical scholars down to the present day. Is it a *personal* question about how all this fits into one's own spiritual life, or an *ecclesial* question about trends and practices in the church, or a *societal* question about the problems that face us in the world today? All of these are good and valid questions, but the type of answer given will depend on the type of question being asked and the resources available for an adequate response.

All of these questions will come into play in what follows, but the plan of this book is built around the distinction between historical and theological questions. After some initial questions on the sources and their interpretation, we will consider questions which have only historical answers (Jesus' life and ministry). Then we will ask questions that move from historical to theological concerns, both the early church's interpretation of Jesus grounded in the cross and resurrection and the later church's continuing interpretation of Jesus in the form of creeds and councils (doctrines). Finally, we will consider questions around the theme of Jesus' significance for today.

In putting questions to Jesus directly or formulating questions about him, we should keep ever present to our minds and alive in our hearts the most central and fundamental question, the one he asks of us as his disciples: "But who do you say that I am?" (Mk 8:29).

FORMAT

THE 101 QUESTIONS AND RESPONSES

Q. 1. If the gospels are an interpretation and have themselves been interpreted over the centuries, how do we know we are in touch with the "real" Jesus?

The same question might be asked of any human relationship. When we meet another person, we immediately enter into a process of interpretation. Initially, we seek certain basic data, e.g. name, background, interests, etc. But at the same time we are sifting and evaluating both the data and the person who is communicating it to us. Without some such process we cannot enter into any personal relationship. However, if we would come to know the "real" person, there comes a point in the relationship when we must move beyond such "factual" information and entrust ourselves to the other in an act of self-transcendence. This can be called an act of faith in the most basic and fundamental sense of that word, i.e. trust.

What is true of every human relationship is true of our relationship with God, with this qualification—that the initiative which makes such trust or faith on our part possible comes from God (and so we call faith an experience of grace). Nonetheless, it is a divine invitation that calls for our human response. As we respond, whether in a relationship with other human persons or with God, the process of interpretation continues or we would never deepen and develop the relationship. In a word, our primary relationship to the God we know in Jesus is one of faith. This is the "real" Jesus. Yet, as with every relationship, such a faith experience gives rise to as many questions as people can ask, e.g. historical, psychological, theological, personal, etc. (cf. Introduction). Not only are these good and valid questions, they are necessary if we are to grow and mature in our faith.

Q. 2. But why couldn't God have made it easier, e.g. why didn't Jesus write the Bible instead of his disciples?

This question must be answered on two levels, first with regard to the nature of Christianity and second with regard to the nature of the Bible. Christianity, unlike Islam, is not a religion of "the book." It is a religion that centers on personal relationships. One need only read the gospel of John to see this. What is important about John is its constant evocation of Jesus' personal relation to the Father (as at 1:18 where Jesus is pictured as existing always in the bosom of the Father) and his invitation to us to enter into that same relationship through the power of the Spirit (as at 13:23 where the disciple whom Jesus loved is pictured as resting in the bosom of Jesus). Whether everything in the gospel of John is historically factual or not, it certainly captures the essence of Christianity: through faith we are caught up into a personal relationship with the triune God that has eternal consequences. This God is alive, active, and present in our hearts and in the very center of all our human relationships. This is the God we celebrate in the person of Jesus.

Scriptures, such as the gospel of John, are a written testimony or witness to this dynamic relationship. All the scriptures bear witness to something prior and more fundamental, namely to the "God of the living" (Mk 12:27) who is constantly raising us to new life within the communal experiences of praise and worship, hearing and proclaiming, breaking and sharing, feeding and clothing. The Bible was written out of just such experiences as these, and it becomes effective in our lives when we are inspired to go and do likewise. Thus, God could not make it easier. The God revealed in Jesus offers us an invitation to life but we must respond in faith and take responsibility by making Jesus' way our own.

Q. 3. Well then, did Jesus say and do all the things the NT writers claim? And, if not, why would they put words into his mouth or make up stories about his great deeds?

This question brings us back to the issue of the "real" Jesus. It is helpful to distinguish three possible meanings of that term. First, there is the Jesus who actually said and did specific things on very specific occasions. We have virtually no access to this Jesus since he wrote nothing himself and the gospels are not biographies in the modern sense of collecting and recording specific items of information.

Second, there is the "historical" Jesus, i.e. the Jesus who can be reconstructed through the critical methods of historical scholarship. Our access to this Jesus is limited but important. We can through critical analysis know certain distinctive ways he had of acting and speaking, e.g. his proclamation of the kingdom of God in parables and his celebration of the kingdom's presence by eating and drinking with tax collectors and sinners. Such reconstruction is heavily dependent on the memory impression of the earliest Christian communities. As with any great historical figure, e.g. Socrates or Lincoln or Kennedy, such memory is based in historical reality but is highly selective and tends to focus upon the "memorable moments," thus excluding either as forgotten or seemingly unimportant specific, concrete details such as the exact time or place of a particular event. Much of the gospel materials were undoubtedly dependent on this kind of selective memory—the community gathered in worship recalling the memorable moments, the impact he had, the incisiveness of his words and the overwhelming power of his deeds—recalling but also embellishing and developing as do all good story-tellers to bring out the deeper truth that was in him.

Finally, there is the biblical Christ: the one proclaimed and interpreted through citations from the Old Testament, through theological reflection on his significance, and above all through the continuing experience of his presence in the power of the Spirit. This last is most important for understanding what the NT writers were doing. As there were prophets inspired by the Spirit in the OT who could say: "Thus says the Lord . . ." so there were prophets in the early communities of Christians who would stand up in the assembly and pronounce a word of the risen Jesus. Inspiration has to do primarily with the community gathered in the power of the Spirit. The written text depends upon and reflects this more fundamental experience of the living voice of the risen Jesus.

Q. 4. But why should I believe that something is true if it didn't really happen?

Your question raises what for most moderns is the biggest obstacle to understanding the scriptures. Most of us, children of the enlightenment which began in the eighteenth century as a movement to free human reason from the tentacles of dogmatic thinking, would subscribe to the proposition: "If it didn't happen, it isn't true." The empirical mind-set, the demand for scientific or historical "proof" as the litmus-test of reality, is so much a part of the furniture of our minds that we are scarcely aware of it. Yet the "truest" things in life are frequently things that never happened or that are not subject to empirical verification. When you read a novel, it is true even though nothing in the novel ever happened as described. It is true because it touches the deepest symbolic levels of human experience; it is true because it enlightens the mind and moves the heart, because it resonates with what is deepest and best in us and calls forth a response that is often too deep to express adequately.

This is the kind of impact that Jesus had on his contemporaries and upon subsequent generations to the present day. For example, what is true about Jesus stilling the storm (Mk 4:35–41) and walking on the water (Mk 6:45–52) is not the rather odd empirical fact of Jesus contravening the laws of nature but the more important *fact* that Jesus both then and now calls us to faith in the midst of life's storms and brings peace into our hearts. That will always remain true whether Jesus ever walked on the water or not. When we read scripture, then, we must learn to think symbolically and not always be preoccupied with just the facts. Truth is too important to be reduced to literal-mindedness.

Q. 5. If the gospels are primarily faith documents that communicate symbolic truths, why do we need the historical Jesus at all? Can't we just stay with Matthew, Mark, Luke, and John?

Indeed we can and should stay with the four gospels. They remain our primary source for whatever we say or think about Jesus. One could spend a lifetime exploring the riches of any one of them. But your question touches on a problem that plagues many today: whether the historical Jesus has any relevance or importance for Christian faith.

The problem is really twofold. The first has to do with the question of method. Given the limitations of historical method as that is understood today, is it possible to know anything at all about the historical Jesus? Without going into details here about methodological debates, I would simply submit to you that we have as much, if not more, reasonably adequate historical information about Jesus as about any historical figure from the distant past.

The second aspect of the problem raises the question of necessity. Is knowledge of the historical Jesus necessary for Christian faith? The answer can vary depending on whether it corresponds to the scholarly or popular level. On the popular level, one can lead a rich and profoundly spiritual Christian life with the sort of traditional faith-image of Jesus outlined in the Introduction. But if one begins to ask the kind of historical questions about sources and interpretations that we are asking here, one is inevitably led into the views and approaches of modern scholarship.

In my view, knowledge of the historical Jesus functions in a subordinate but indispensable way in relation to the knowledge we have of Jesus in faith. It is *subordinate* because our primary relationship to Jesus is one of faith. This faith is communicated to us through such communities as those represented by Matthew, Mark, Luke, and John as well as the Christian communities of the last two millennia. It is a faith personally appropriated by each of us in the context of our own personal and communal experiences. Knowledge of the historical Jesus is *indispensable* for the simple reason that Christian faith has always been grounded in the historical particularity of the man Jesus from Nazareth. What we do know of him historically helps to make more concrete our faith-image of him. What would our image of Jesus be like if we had only the letters of Paul and not the four gospels? But, perhaps more importantly, historical knowledge functions in a negative way to limit or control what we might say about him. The danger of subsequent interpretations has always been to re-create Jesus in one's own image, e.g. as imperial Lord, leftist revolutionary, liberal free-thinker, etc. The only response to and control of such images is to appeal to what we know of him historically.

Q. 6. Haven't the scholars made Jesus inaccessible? How can an ordinary person come to know and understand all these latest developments in biblical criticism?

We should never forget that our faith is a communal faith. Christian faith should never be viewed as involving a group of isolated individuals doing their own thing. Each of us is a member of a believing community. Each of us has been nourished by the community so as to grow in faith and each of us is expected to contribute our own faith and talents to the community's continued growth and development. St. Paul calls the Christian community a body that has many members, all of whom are important to the well-being of the whole. "The eye cannot say to the hand, 'I have no need of you,' nor again the head to the feet, 'I have no need of you' " (1 Cor 12:21; see the whole of chapter 12 as well as Rom 12:3–8). The whole point of the "base Christian communities" in Latin America (and now spread throughout the world) is to enable all persons in the community to find their own voice, i.e. to express their own experience of faith in the concrete interaction of contemporary reality and their reading of scripture. It would be a tragedy if people left the reading of the scriptures to the scholars alone.

Yet the scholars too are members of the community and have their contribution to make. Conflicts arise only if scholars set themselves in opposition to the community. Even then we can learn much from voices that are critical, especially about our own honesty in seeking the truth. In any event, we should not wait for the latest developments in scholarly research before we take up the church's witness in the scriptures and immerse ourselves in them. On the other hand, as we read, questions will inevitably arise. Scholars can help us greatly in our ongoing task of interpretation and indeed are indispensable to the community's self-understanding. Like the Ethiopian eunuch, we do not always understand what we are reading and need someone to interpret (Acts 8:26–39).

Q. 7. Why are there so many different views of Jesus today?

The question touches on the issue of pluralism. We live in a culture that is profoundly aware of differing viewpoints and approaches, of differences in races, cultures, traditions, histories, languages, religions, etc. Increasingly, we live in a culture that is also sensitively aware that such differences are good and legitimate. The image of the "melting pot" is being replaced by the multi-colored rainbow. The tendency of the dominant culture toward uniformity is being challenged. There should always be a healthy tension between unity and plurality, in the church as well as in society. The extreme of uniformity leads to totalitarianism; the extreme of separateness and division leads to fanaticism. Both have their root in a desire for dominance and a fear of the truth that makes us free (Jn 8:32).

While we may be more acutely aware of the reality and the legitimacy of pluralism today, we should also recognize that a legitimate pluralism has always existed in the church. For example, in contrast to past attempts to "harmonize" the four gospels into one "life" of Jesus, which in effect was to produce a fifth gospel which did not correspond to any of the original four, we now recognize more clearly that the gospels of Mark, Matthew, Luke, and John all give us a distinctive picture of Jesus born out of the faith experience of each respective community. And indeed it should be so, for the mystery that is Jesus cannot be reduced to or encapsulated in any one faith experience, be that communal or individual. The mystery of his person will always transcend our attempts, even biblical and creedal attempts, to bring him to expression in human language. Thus, we can expect differences but not contradictions. The four gospels give us different views of Jesus, but they do not contradict each other. Like a diamond held up to the light, Jesus reflects and reveals the glory of God in many and diverse ways.

Q. 8. Why is Jesus portrayed in so many paintings and statues as a white man with blond hair and blue eyes when he actually was Jewish?

There are two dimensions of Jesus that we should never forget. First, on the historical level, he was a first century Palestinian Jew. The Jewishness of Jesus is extremely important for Christian faith. Jesus was a man of his people and of his times. He connects us with the rich and wondrous tradition that begins with the faith of our common father Abraham. Anti-Jewish prejudice, and the pogroms that have tragically too often taken place in Christian history, are anti-Jesus. If we believe in Jesus, we accept as our own the heritage of being Jewish, and we revere that heritage as expressive of God's will for us.

Yet, secondly, Jesus the man of his times is also the man for all times. On the theological level he has become the second Adam (1 Cor 15:20–22.45–49; Rom 5:14ff), the new human being who embodies and embraces all of humanity. This means that he is not only a white man with blond hair and blue eyes (as often represented in western European art) but he is also, as risen, Greek as well as Jew, free as well as slave, female as well as male (Gal 3:28). He is African, Asian, Latin as well as European and North American. He is the "Apache Christ" as well as the "cosmic Christ." As the poet Gerard Manley Hopkins has put it:

... Christ plays in ten thousand places,
Lovely in limbs, and lovely in eyes not his
To the Father through the features of men's faces.

Q. 9. Why has it taken so long to come to study and appreciate the humanity of Jesus?

It is true that the traditional image of Jesus has tended to lay greater stress on his divinity. Because we believe that he is God, his humanity has always been something of a problem. Already in the community which gave us the gospel of John, with its great stress on Jesus' eternal relation to the Father, we see this problem emerging. The author of the first letter of John has to insist that "Jesus Christ has come in the flesh" (4:2). The letter condemns those who do not accept Jesus' flesh and blood humanity. The early fathers and councils, much influenced by the gospel of John, struggled with the same issue. They insisted that Jesus was fully human because he could not save us if he did not assume our full human nature, i.e. a human body and soul. The only problem with this is that his humanity too often appeared to be only an abstract "principle of being" which had to be affirmed for the sake of our salvation. The living, vibrant, flesh and blood human being like us in all things (Heb 4:15) was not the focus of their theological interest.

What the so-called "quest of the historical Jesus" (which began around 1778 and continues to the present) has given us is a Jesus with a more human face. With the development of our modern historical consciousness, we have become more sensitive to the central importance of the human and historical in Jesus' life as well as in our own. We are more attracted to one who had to struggle, grow, and learn as we do; to one who has felt what we feel, suffered what we suffer; to one who knows from within the joys and the hopes, the griefs and the anxieties of our common human lot, especially those who are poor or in any way afflicted (see the opening of Vatican II's Pastoral Constitution on the Church in the Modern World). In contrast to earlier times, today we lay greater stress on his humanity than on his divinity. A balanced view will always affirm with the Council of Chalcedon the fullness of both humanity and divinity.

Q. 10. Do we know more about Jesus than he knew about himself?

In a sense, the answer to this must be both yes and no. There are many things we do not know about Jesus. We do not know what he looked like, what personal likes or dislikes he had, how his life developed in terms of a chronological sequence of events or of psychological growth. There are many such historical particulars that we would dearly love to know, but they are lost in the mists of time. Yet, on the other hand, we do know more about him than he could have known within the limitations of his human, historical life. For we view him from the revealing light of the resurrection and the developed interpretations of the faith community under the guidance of the Spirit, both in scripture and in creed. The Nicene Creed that we say every Sunday in church is the expression of a mature faith that has had the benefit of what I would call the "whole" experience of Jesus, i.e. his human and historical life, his death on the cross, his resurrection, and the church's reflection upon and deepening appropriation of the mystery that is Jesus. Yet, the Nicene Creed, like the scriptures, is a limited expression in human language of a mystery that simply transcends our capabilities. So, while we can say yes, we do know more about Jesus than he knew about himself, we can turn the question around and say that Jesus as risen Lord in the eternal embrace of the Father knows far more about himself and indeed about us than we could ever imagine.

Q. 11. Are the stories about Jesus' conception and birth true?

One must answer with an unequivocal yes. They are true insofar as they are the valid expression of the faith of those communities represented by the first two chapters of the gospels of Luke and Matthew respectively. They are true as two independent and indeed quite different affirmations of the religious truth about Jesus: that he is (1) the Son of God conceived by the power of the Holy Spirit in the virgin Mary, and (2) the Son of David through his father Joseph who was descended from the house and family of David. The primary import of the infancy narratives is to communicate the same religious truth that was stated earlier by Paul, who in turn was citing one of the earliest Christian creeds: ". . . the gospel concerning his

[God's] Son, who was descended from David according to the flesh and was declared to be Son of God with power according to the Spirit of holiness by resurrection from the dead, Jesus Christ our Lord . . ." (Rom 1:3–4). The stories about Jesus' conception and birth, which by the way are found in the whole of the NT *only* in Matthew and Luke, are primarily intended to convey the basic faith convictions of the early Christian communities in the light of the resurrection. Therefore, they must be understood along with the whole of scripture as primarily religious in nature.

But your question is more likely asking about historical or factual truth. A careful reading of the two accounts both in themselves and in relation to one another shows that they cannot be completely historical and that they are primarily concerned about religious truth. However, at least minimally, we could say the following is historical: Jesus was born in Bethlehem of Judea (but possibly in Nazareth) during the latter years of the reign of King Herod the Great (therefore sometime around 6–4 B.C.E.). His father's name was Joseph and his mother's name was Mary. He was called Jesus and was always known to be from Nazareth in Galilee. These elements are confirmed by other texts outside the infancy narratives and are generally accepted as historically probable.

Q. 12. But what about the fact that Jesus was born of a virgin? Isn't that historical?

Both Matthew 1:18–25 and Luke 1:26–38 affirm unequivocally, though Luke less clearly than Matthew, that Jesus was *conceived* by a virgin named Mary. Luke's account does not necessarily exclude the intervention of a human father; it simply ignores it. The important point is that through the power of God's Spirit "the child to be born will be holy; he will be called Son of God" (Lk 1:35). Matthew, on the other hand, clearly excludes the human father. Mary is presented as an unwed mother whom Joseph plans to dismiss because of her pregnancy. Only a revelation from God, namely: "the child conceived in her is from the Holy Spirit" (Mt 1:20), prevents him from doing so. Luke's account might conceivably find its parallel in the accounts of other OT figures whose conception was deemed miraculous, e.g. Samuel (Mary's "Magnificat" is largely based on Hannah's prayer in 1 Sam 2:1–10). Why then does Matthew wish to make the point so strongly? One possible explanation is that Matthew is engaging in a polemic (argument) against Jewish adversaries to Christianity. At the end of Matthew's gospel there is a clear polemic against those who claimed that the disciples had stolen Jesus' body from the tomb (Mt 27:62–66; 28:11–15). A similar polemic against those who questioned Jesus' origins may also be present at the beginning of the gospel. Whether there was a clear charge of illegitimacy this early among Jewish opponents is not clear from the NT; it does clearly appear by around 150 C.E. In any event, Matthew's concern in chapter 1 is twofold: to affirm that Jesus is Son of David through Joseph by tracing his genealogy from Abraham through David to Joseph (vv. 1–17) and that he is Messiah, Savior, Emmanuel (he does not use Son of God at this point) through the creative action of the Holy Spirit (vv. 18–25). This is the theological or religious truth of both accounts.

As to the question of history, we meet here the limits of historical methods. History can neither affirm nor deny the fact of Jesus' virginal conception. Its truth comes from another dimension, namely that of revelation. Note that within the stories themselves, the possibility of such knowledge depends on revelation. In Matthew's account, an angel of the Lord appeared to Joseph in a dream; in Luke's account, the angel Gabriel appears to Mary. This indicates once again that the concerns of both authors are religious and theological, not historical.

Q. 13. Well then, did Mary and Joseph know Jesus was the Son of God when he was born?

Probably not, but we do. What I mean by that, once again, is that the infancy narratives of Matthew and Luke are not strictly speaking historical accounts, though they may contain some historical memories as mentioned earlier. In spite of many theories and hypotheses that have been developed over the centuries, the simple fact is that we do not know what sources Matthew and Luke had at their disposal. We do know that the two infancy narratives are strik-

ingly different accounts and that they are heavily laden with religious and theological interests. We also know that they agree on
the most essential point of Christian faith, namely that Jesus as Son
of God was conceived by the Holy Spirit and born of the Virgin
Mary. This remains eternally true whatever was the actual personal
experience of Mary and Joseph. To say that Mary and Joseph probably did not know that he was the Son of God at the time of his birth
but that we do is to say that we view the life of Jesus from the
privileged perspective of our resurrection faith. We know, as it were,
the whole story.

Does this mean that we should reject the infancy narratives as
"just stories"? By no means. Such a reaction betrays the attitude of
mind that equates historical fact with truth. People have lived for
centuries, as we do every Christmas, the wonderful truth of
Matthew's and Luke's infancy narratives. They are true because
they touch what is deepest in our hearts and give us new life and
hope. They are even more true because they proclaim in concrete
and moving images who Jesus of Nazareth really was and is at the
very center of his being.

Q. 14. What about the fact that Jesus is said to have existed before time? How could he be eternal and still be born?

Your question moves us to the origins of Jesus as presented in
the gospel of John. It is worth noting again that besides Matthew and
Luke the rest of the NT (including Paul with his high Christology)
shows no knowledge of or at least no interest in the narratives of
Jesus' conception and birth. This is particularly striking in John
who affirms so strongly Jesus' divine origins. The only direct reference to Jesus' birth occurs at the trial before Pilate: "For this I was
born, and for this I came into the world, to testify to the truth" (Jn
18:37). It may be implied in another rather violent controversy section when Jesus' adversaries say: "We were not born illegitimate!"
(8:41; tr. mine), but the concern of John is to transcend such preoc-
cupations about Jesus' earthly origins, for in fact he comes from
God. Thus, he says of himself in the same section: "Before Abraham
was, I am" (8:58). The gospel of John is concerned about Jesus'

eternal relation to the Father, not his earthly origins either at birth or at baptism. It is interesting to note that John has no narrative of the baptism either, but he does have the confession of John the Baptist twice repeated: "This was he of whom I said, 'He who comes after me ranks ahead of me because he was before me' " (1:15.30). Jesus exists before John the Baptist, before Abraham, indeed before the creation of the world as the Word who was God (1:1–5). While John also affirms that "the Word became flesh and lived among us" (1:14), he makes no attempt to relate that affirmation to any narratives about his conception and birth.

Thus, with regard to the scriptural witness, there are at least four distinct traditions about Jesus' origins as the Son of God: (1) constituted or declared such at the resurrection (Rom 1:4); (2) at the baptism (Mk 1:10–11); (3) at his conception and birth (Mt 1:20; Lk 1:35); (4) before creation (Jn 1:1–5; 17:5). With artless simplicity, these traditions are left standing side by side without any attempt to resolve or harmonize the tensions between them. That was left to later generations. It is we who seek to bring together the prologue of John and the infancy narratives of Matthew and Luke.

Q. 15. According to your principle of ongoing interpretation, that's all right, isn't it? But I've always wondered what it means in the Creed when it says that Jesus was "begotten, not made."

Your observation is right on target. I wanted to clarify what the scriptures say in response to the preceding question, but it is certainly true that the church continued right on after the biblical period interpreting the mystery. Indeed, the first seven ecumenical councils from 325 to 787 were all convoked primarily to resolve questions that revolved around the significance of Jesus.

The first ecumenical council at Nicea in 325 was concerned about the teaching of a popular and well-known priest from Alexandria named Arius. His influence was very strong and continues to some degree even to the present day. Arius, following the normal understanding of Greek philosophy at the time, maintained that if someone is born or becomes flesh, that person is a creature. To say that "the Word became flesh" is to say that the Son of God is a creature, albeit the first and primary creature in God's plan. The council took an ancient baptismal profession of faith in the Father–Son–Holy Spirit and inserted four statements about the Son aimed explicitly at Arius. The council affirmed that "the one Lord Jesus Christ, the Son of God" is (1) "begotten of the Father . . . that is, of the being of the Father": against any idea that he was begotten from the Father as a creature in time; (2) "true God of true God": against any idea that he was a lesser or inferior god, i.e. divine but not truly and fully God; (3) "begotten, not made": against the common understanding that the two are the same, so that to be begotten is to be made or created; (4) "of the same being [*homoousion*] as the Father": the famous word *homoousion* was adopted, as was the preceding distinction between "begotten" and "made," contrary to the usual understanding of the word. It was considered useful to maintain the full divinity of Jesus. With all four statements against Arius, the council is affirming that Jesus is truly begotten by the Father but within the eternal dynamic of God's very being.

It should be noted that the fathers did not attempt in the creedal statement itself to explain *how* Jesus could be eternally begotten of the Father and still be born in time. The Creed simply goes on to state the biblical affirmations of his becoming human, suffering, rising, and ascending into heaven "for us humans and for our salvation." The question of "how" has continued to exercise theological minds from that day to this. One problem created by the creedal statement is the apparent, though perhaps unintended, separation of Jesus' eternal relation to the Father and his appearance in time.

Finally, it should be mentioned that the Creed we say every Sunday, while often called the Nicene Creed, is in fact a different and longer Creed that was formulated at the second ecumenical council in Constantinople in 381. It does repeat the same basic affirmations against Arius as the Council of Nicea, but its major concern was to affirm the full divinity of the Holy Spirit against those who were denying it. Thus, with Constantinople I we have the official definition of the triune nature of God, a definition based in the continuing practice of baptizing in the name of the Father and the Son and the Holy Spirit (Mt 28:19).

Q. 16. Coming back for the moment to Jesus' infancy and childhood, who named Jesus? What does "Jesus" mean and where did the name "Jesus Christ" come from?

According to Matthew 1:25, Joseph named Jesus following the directive of the angel (1:21). According to Luke 1:31, the angel Gabriel speaking to Mary says: "You will name him Jesus." Later at the circumcision Luke simply says: "He was called Jesus, the name given by the angel before he was conceived in the womb" (2:21). Thus, according to both Matthew and Luke, God through angelic revelation named Jesus. In any event, Jesus was a relatively common name at that time. It comes from the Hebrew for Joshua (*Yehošua',* later shortened to *Yešua'* and *Yešu*). It may have originally meant "Yahweh helps" but was later interpreted in popular usage as "Yahweh saves." Thus, the angel says to Joseph: ". . . you are to name him Jesus, for he will save his people from their sins" (Mt 1:21).

Historically, Jesus would have been known as *Yešu bar Yosef* = Jesus son of Joseph. Theologically, he came to be known as "the Christ" from the Greek *ho christos,* which means "the anointed" and translates the Hebrew *ha mašiah* or Messiah. Originally, Christ was one of the many titles applied to Jesus by the early church in the light of the resurrection. Gradually, as other titles became more predominant and as the church moved out of Palestine where the title was more easily understood within its Hebrew environment and into the larger Greco-Roman cultural and linguistic setting, "Christ" tended more and more to be employed as part of Jesus' proper name. But, we should always remember that during his own lifetime his proper name was *Yešu bar Yosef.*

Q. 17. Did Jesus have brothers and sisters?

Mark 6:3 (cp. Mt 13:55–56) says: "Is not this the carpenter, the son of Mary and brother of James and Joses and Judas and Simon, and are not his sisters here with us?" It is mentioned that his mother and brothers and sisters came looking for him (Mk 3:31–35 par.). John pictures his mother and brothers as accompanying him in his ministry at times (Jn 2:12; 7:3.5). The brothers seem to have had some prominence in the early church (Acts 1:14; 1 Cor 9:5), especially James who was the leader of the early community at Jerusalem (Gal 1:19; Acts 15:13–21). It is particularly significant that Paul refers to James as the Lord's brother. This is someone he knew personally. Would he have singled him out with this designation if he had any reason to think otherwise? Thus, one possible meaning of the biblical texts is that Jesus did indeed have brothers and sisters. Jesus himself is designated as the "firstborn male" (Lk 2:23), but this does not necessarily imply brothers and sisters.

Later post-biblical interpretations, particularly in the fourth century, have sought alternative explanations. One maintained that Jesus' brothers were half-brothers (a possible meaning of the Greek word *adelphos:* see Mk 6:17) by reason of an earlier marriage of Joseph. The only problem with this is that there is no evidence of such a previous marriage. A more plausible interpretation is that Jesus' brothers and sisters were really cousins. St. Jerome advocated this interpretation based on the Hebrew word for brother (*'āh*), which can also mean cousin or any close relative (e.g. Gn 14:16; 29:15; Lv 10:14). These texts were translated in the Greek version of the OT (known as the Septuagint) as *adelphos* (= brother) even though Greek does have a distinct word for cousin (*anepsios* as at Col 4:10). It is quite conceivable that Paul, coming as he did from a strong semitic background, would have spontaneously used *adelphos* for James in the sense of a cousin or close relation.

On purely biblical grounds, arguments from linguistic usage alone would admit either of the above interpretations. The gospels were concerned to preserve the virginal conception of Jesus (see q. 12). After biblical times, and particularly in the fourth century with the monastic idealization of the state of virginity, Mary who had always been revered in both popular and official piety became by reason of her perpetual virginity the central and supreme symbol or model of that state of life. There is nothing in scripture that denies the possibility of her perpetual virginity, and it is difficult to imagine how such a devotion could have arisen if it was popularly thought

that Jesus had brothers and sisters as we normally understand
the terms.

**Q. 18. Why is Mary so important? Sometimes it seems that more
attention is given to her than to Jesus.**

Mary is a powerful symbol of what is deepest and best in Christian faith. People sometimes say: "It's just a symbol, therefore not
real." Symbols are real, the most real of human experiences for we
would not be human at all without symbols. We communicate symbolically. Our language is symbolic. True symbols have power because they evoke the deepest levels of human experience and awareness, not only individually but collectively, not only now but
throughout human history. To say that Jesus and Mary are powerful
symbols is to affirm their central and decisive importance for all of
humankind.

C.G. Jung, the great psychologist of the collective unconscious,
thought that the doctrine of the immaculate conception (defined in
1854) was of decisive importance because, on the psychological
level, it located the feminine within the divine. Of course, in the past
Protestants have often accused Catholics of making Mary a goddess,
and this has occurred at times in the popular imagination. But we
can find common agreement in the NT. There Mary's importance is
always in relationship to Jesus and, of course, it is primarily based in
the fact that she is his mother. Recently there have been many attempts to try to rediscover the "historical" Mary of Nazareth, and
some powerful images have emerged that might otherwise be overlooked: unwed mother (Mt 1:18–19); refugee woman with child (Mt
2:13–15); widow; mother of an innocent man persecuted and killed
by the imperial powers, etc. Like Jesus, such images resonate in the
experience of the poor and the persecuted. Above all, she is seen as a
woman of faith willing to follow her son even to the cross.

But for Luke and John—the two authors who manifest the
greatest interest in Mary—her symbolic importance is primarily as
the embodiment of her people Israel. In Luke's infancy narrative,
the parallel annunciations about John the Baptist and Jesus culminate in Mary's journey to Elizabeth: the "Magnificat" is a song of

liberation for God's "servant Israel." The parallel births likewise culminate in another journey, this time to the temple when Jesus was twelve. The image of Mary treasuring all these words and pondering them in her heart when the shepherds visit (2:19) is repeated at the end of the scene in the temple (2:51). For Luke, God's fulfillment of the promises to Israel, which is the main theme of the infancy narrative, is realized in Mary. She is the one who clearly embodies the hopes and dreams of her people. She is not only the mother of Jesus; through him she is the mother of her people Israel. A similar image is present, it seems to me, in John's gospel. At the wedding feast of Cana (2:1–11), early in the gospel, Mary anticipates the hopes of all Israel that Jesus' "hour" would come (the wine is a symbol of the hoped-for blessings of salvation). When the hour has finally come, at the end of the gospel, Jesus on the cross (19:25–27) entrusts his mother (Israel) to "the disciple whom he loved" (symbol of the church as the new Israel). Israel has now found her true home.

As Mary is symbol of Israel, so she has become for us symbol of the church. In her we see fulfilled our deepest hopes and dreams, from her immaculate conception to her assumption into heaven. We should always have a profound devotion to her but, as she herself would have it, in order to celebrate more fully the central and decisive significance of her son.

Q. 19. You mentioned that Mary was a widow. Whatever happened to Joseph?

In Matthew's infancy narrative Joseph is the central figure to whom are given the revelations, but in Luke, Mary is central and Joseph is a more peripheral figure. The differences reflect theological concerns: Jesus' lineage from Joseph in Matthew, Mary's embodiment of Israel in Luke. The last we hear of Joseph in Matthew is that "he made his home in a town called Nazareth" (2:23), apparently for the first time according to this gospel, while Jesus was still young. In Luke, he and Mary search for Jesus in the temple in Jerusalem when Jesus was twelve years old. Jesus returned to Nazareth with his parents and "was obedient to them" (2:51). Since Jesus' mother and brothers and sisters are mentioned during the public ministry but Joseph is not, we can only surmise that Joseph died sometime between Jesus' twelfth and thirtieth year. Hence, Mary became a widow. Popular piety has always had a great devotion to Joseph, and indeed it should. But we know no more about him than what the scriptures give us.

Q. 20. Matthew and Luke don't seem to tell us much about Jesus' childhood and teenage life. Are there any historically accurate accounts about that time in his life?

No. The only reliable accounts are those contained in the canonical gospels written sometime between 70 and 100 C.E. In postbiblical times there emerged a number of Christian writings, some called "gospels," which were not accepted into the NT. Catholics call them "apocrypha" and Protestants "pseudepigrapha." They are considered "false writings" in the sense that they are not accepted as correct or accurate expressions of the Christian faith. On the other hand, they contain much material that has had great influence on Christian piety. For example, the Gospel of James (*Protoevangelium Jacobi*), written in the second century, has been one of the most influential as it contains rather fanciful accounts of Joachim and Anna, Mary's parents, along with the story of Mary's birth, betrothal to Joseph, etc. While interesting, such a writing also shows the danger of allowing free rein to the fanciful imagination when sources are lacking and also the danger of mixing together in the popular mind the quite distinct accounts of Matthew and Luke.

Another very influential work from the second century is *The Infancy Gospel of Thomas,* which also tries to fill the gaps in Jesus' childhood up to the age of twelve. Its popularity may seem surprising to us as Jesus is presented as an insufferable, ill-tempered little brat who decides on a whim to kill or to heal. It does have the value of telling us how we should *not* imagine the childhood of Jesus. Jesus' early years lie hidden in the silent solidarity of one who walked with his people some thirty years before he ever spoke a public word. Legitimate historical questions about those years can only appeal to his public words and deeds, plus our general knowledge of the times and culture in which he lived.

Q. 21. When did Jesus know he was God's Son? As a baby or a child or a teenager or later?

This is similar to the question about Mary's and Joseph's knowledge of him, but of course more central to our faith as it touches the way we view his human life. Raymond E. Brown puts the matter well: "The Gospels were written to tell us what *we* should know of Jesus, not what he knew of himself." We know in the light of resurrection faith that he was God's Son not only at the moment of his conception but eternally in the bosom of the Father (Jn 1:18). Nonetheless, when we do ask such questions about Jesus' own knowledge, we should be clear that we are asking about his *human* knowledge, not his divine knowledge. The mystery, of course, is how Jesus can be fully human and not be overpowered by his divinity.

If we are asking an historical question about Jesus' own psychological development, we have no access to what went on in his own mind. Whatever it was, he seems not to have communicated it during the years at Nazareth. According to Mark his own family tried to restrain him because they thought he was out of his mind (3:21). His friends and neighbors at Nazareth rejected him on the grounds that they knew him too well: "Where did this man get all this? . . . Is not this the carpenter, the son of Mary . . . ?" (6:2–3). If we affirm as does the letter to the Hebrews that Jesus was like us in all things, tested or tempted as we are (4:15), then we should say that he grew up like a normal child, becoming strong and increasing in wisdom and in years and in favor with both God and humans (Lk 2:40.52).

On the other hand, the question is usually posed in theological terms. If he was God, then in his human knowledge he must have had the beatific vision and infused divine knowledge as well as normal, human experiential knowledge. This is the view of Thomas Aquinas and has been the predominant view until recent times. In my own view, such an approach is unnecessary and indeed damaging, for it effectively robs Jesus of his full humanness as one who walked with his people, experienced what they experienced, suffered what they suffered, knew from inside as it were the possibilities but also the limitations of being human. Whatever we say of Jesus' divinity, it should affirm and not deny the full range of his human experience as a fellow sojourner who had to face the reality of death just as we do.

Q. 22. Can we say that Jesus was a leader in his youth as he was later as an adult?

We can certainly imagine that the qualities which he manifested during his public ministry were already present and developing during the years at Nazareth. From all we know, those years were quiet and uneventful, yet in spite of his later rejection by the people of Nazareth it does appear that some of his family and friends did follow him, e.g. his "brother" James. Some of those who followed him from other villages may have known him earlier. Certainly, the power he had came primarily from his anointing with the Spirit at his baptism. Yet that power expressed itself through his human personality, which from the gospel accounts we might characterize in the following terms.

He was a religiously faithful Jew yet free enough to know that the law was meant to serve human flourishing. He was very observant of detail and noticed with sympathetic understanding the foibles and ironies of human life. He was compassionate and reached out to embrace the excluded: the sick and possessed, the despised and marginalized, the poor and dispossessed, women, children, foreigners. He loved nature and the God who made the lilies of the field and the birds of the air. He was decisive and did not hesitate to call a spade a spade, especially when it came to hypocrisy. He knew how to celebrate and loved a good meal with his friends. He also knew what it meant to discipline himself and to prepare for the trials to come. He knew how to pray and is said to have spent whole nights alone with God. He surely in all this knew how to smile. Is this leadership? Yes indeed, if a leader is one who inspires others, literally gives them his own spirit, so that they are enabled to go forth and live empowered by that same spirit.

Q. 23. Do we know anything about Jesus' education? What kind of education did he receive? Also, how many languages did he know?

With regard to spoken language, Jesus could have known Aramaic, Hebrew, Latin, and Greek, as all were used in first century Palestine. Without going into the detailed arguments, it seems likely that his normal, everyday language was Aramaic which is similar to Hebrew and had replaced it as the common language of the Jewish people living in Palestine. He probably knew some Hebrew from attending synagogue services and hearing the sacred scriptures. Greek was the common language of trade and commerce, so he may well have known enough for business purposes. Latin is unlikely in the circles he traveled.

With regard to education, the question is often asked: Could he read and write? Since he was an oral teacher, the texts of the NT manifest little interest and really no hard evidence that he could. The seemingly most obvious text is Lk 4:16–21 when Jesus comes to Nazareth and reads the text of Isaiah, but this text is so oriented to Luke's theological interests that it is hard to know if it is historical as it stands. However, from what we know of his later ministry, especially his ability to enter into debates about the law with the trained scribes, it is clear that he knew the scriptures well. A strong indication is the question his adversaries ask: "How does this man have such learning [literally: know his letters], when he has never been taught?" (Jn 7:15). Two things seem clear: Jesus had no formal training as a scribe learned in the law and he knew his scriptures well. Where did he learn? He probably went to synagogue for rudimentary instruction until the age of twelve and he may have received more formal instruction from his parents and relatives. However, his main schooling would have been in the trade of his father Joseph, i.e. as a carpenter.

Q. 24. Was Jesus really a carpenter? Would this have meant that he belonged to a lower class and was really poor?

In Mark Jesus is referred to directly as "the carpenter," although Matthew reads "the carpenter's son" (13:55) and Luke simply "Joseph's son" (4:22) in the parallel passages. Mark 6:3 is the only text in the entire NT that calls him a carpenter. The word in Greek (*tektōn*) refers in general to one who works with wood or other hard materials and would thus imply a broader range than the English "carpenter." Although it is striking that Jesus never uses images from his trade in his public teaching, there does not seem to be any good reason to deny Mark's report as an historical memory. If Joseph was a carpenter, then Jesus would have simply followed in the trade of his father, a normal and likely occurrence in that culture.

As a carpenter, he would not have been poor in the sense of destitute, like day-laborers. Neither would he have been rich. He would have been a hard-working member of a rural peasant culture. That culture was constituted mostly of farmers from rural villages who would have existed, either by force or by necessity, in some kind of dependent relationship on urban centers ruled by an aristocratic elite (the temple aristocracy and the Roman imperial power). The relative wealth or poverty of the village would have depended on a variety of factors that rural folk know well: weather, prices, taxes, politics, etc. Jesus with his specialized and somewhat technical skill would see his fortunes rise and fall with that of the village.

In addition, the gospels portray Jesus as journeying about in the towns and villages of Galilee and Judea. With the exception of Jerusalem, the larger urban and cosmopolitan centers with their Greco-Roman influence are not mentioned, e.g. Hellenistic cities in Galilee like Tiberias and Sepphoris (the latter a city rebuilt by Herod Antipas and only an hour's walk from Nazareth). Thus, we can imagine Jesus in the early years of his adulthood as a rural peasant, a hard-working and, given the nature of his work, rather muscular young man who had to earn his daily bread by the sweat of his brow and who knew well the small successes and sometimes disastrous setbacks that mark rural life.

Q. 25. Did Jesus ever speak of a sexual desire in his own life? Was he like every teenager who faces this normal urge?

Given the frequently uptight and certainly pervasive preoccupation with sex in our society, it is striking that Jesus rarely speaks to this issue in the records we have. He was more concerned with the quality of human relationships than with the sex act as such. The most direct text occurs in his comment on the sixth commandment as Matthew gives it to us in the sermon on the mount: "You have heard that it was said, 'You shall not commit adultery.' But I say to you that everyone who looks at a woman with lust has already committed adultery with her in his heart" (Mt 5:27–28). This saying, plus the prohibition against divorce that follows (vv. 31–32), has more to do with male attitudes toward women than with individual sex acts. The saying about divorce has to do with a societal practice that was oppressive to women. The saying about adultery has to do with the way men are socialized to view women as mere objects of their drives for pleasure. Jesus had a deep and very sensitive respect for women. In public, he did not ignore them as was the practice of the time; rather he spoke with them and engaged them in conversation. He saw them as imaging the very presence and activity of God. He called them to follow him as disciples. He touched them and healed them and defended them against the male prejudice of a dominant patriarchal society. In a word, he had a very healthy attitude toward and relationship with women.

With regard to the second part of the question, did he smile, laugh, dream, desire? Of course! As a teenager and young man, Jesus was a normal human being who had to learn how to integrate his sexual urges and desires into a mature and balanced personality. To say otherwise is to imply that sex is dirty or somehow sinful. But in God's good creation the differentiation into male and female and their union in one flesh is the culminating expression of God's creativity (see Gn 2:18–24; 1:26–31; brought together by Jesus at Mk 10:6–8 = Mt 19:4–6).

Q. 26. Why didn't Jesus marry? Did he reject this central and important part of human life?

There are some who maintain that Jesus actually did marry. However, since there is absolutely no evidence in favor, the argument must be one from silence, i.e. given no evidence to the contrary one would naturally assume that a Jewish boy by the time he reached the age of eighteen would have been betrothed and married. If Jesus had a normal Jewish upbringing in every other respect, why not in this as well? Certainly any argument against his having a wife and children should not be based on the idea that marriage is somehow a lesser or inferior state of life or that sex is somehow sinful. Given that he lived in Nazareth until about the age of thirty, one might well expect that he would have been married.

However, if that were so one would expect some mention of his wife and children along with his mother and brothers and sisters, as well as many other women, in the public ministry. There is none. In addition, although it is unusual, it is not unheard-of for a man to live a single, celibate life at that time. One need only think of the sectarian movement known as the "Essenes," of the prophet Jeremiah (Jer 16:1-4), of John the Baptist, and of the apostle Paul (1 Cor 7:1-7; 9:5). Given these two factors, it seems most probable that Jesus for whatever reasons chose voluntary celibacy. He certainly was not rejecting or devaluing marriage. We can only conjecture about his reasons from what we know of his public ministry. Two things stand out: he challenged the dominant patriarchal structure of his society (and so perhaps chose not to participate in the privilege and power of a "father's rule" over his family) and he proposed a new family of those who do the will of God (Mk 3:31-35). Thus, it would appear that he made himself a eunuch for the sake of the kingdom of heaven (Mt 19:12).

Q. 27. Are you implying that Jesus abandoned his family? Did he insist on that with the apostles when they later followed him?

If Jesus lived at Nazareth for thirty years, it can scarcely be said that he abandoned anyone, and certainly not his mother and brothers and sisters. Nor did the apostles and his brothers after his death think that they somehow had to live solitary lives apart from their wives and families. Paul refers to this in passing: "Do we not have the right to be accompanied by a believing wife, as do the other apostles and the brothers of the Lord and Cephas?" (1 Cor 9:5).

But, in the gospels, Jesus is presented as a man on a mission with all of his extraordinary powers focused on the one thing necessary: the arrival of the kingdom of God. He seems to have had a two-pronged strategy. He called certain ones (including the twelve as a symbol of a renewed Israel) to follow him, leaving everything to go about in the towns and villages preaching the kingdom and healing the sick and possessed. But not everyone was called to be a disciple in this sense. Most of those who heard him or were healed did not follow him on the way like blind Bartimaeus (Mk 10:52). One indeed who wanted to do so was told: "Go home to your friends, and tell them how much the Lord has done for you . . ." (Mk 5:19). However historical each individual account may be, it seems clear that Jesus had disciples who followed him on the way and others who remained at home and received him when he passed that way, e.g. Martha and Mary (Lk 10:38–42). This may be reflected in the missionary directive: "Whenever you enter a house, stay there until you leave the place" (Mk 6:10). In any case, whether on the road or at home, only one thing is absolutely necessary to human life: "Strive first for the kingdom of God and his righteousness, and all these things will be given to you as well" (Mt 6:33).

Q. 28. Why is celibacy so important? Does the church's insistence on celibacy for priests go back to Jesus?

The only text on celibacy directly attributed to Jesus is the one on those who have made themselves eunuchs for the sake of the kingdom, found only at Matthew 19:12. If this does go back to the historical Jesus, it may represent a certain defense of his own lifestyle. Otherwise, neither he nor his opponents manifest any interest in the question. The important point in the text is that celibacy is freely given and freely accepted: "Not everyone can accept this teaching, but only those to whom it is given" (v. 11). To emphasize the point, this is said before the saying about eunuchs and then repeated at the end: "Let anyone accept this who can" (v. 12d). Similarly, Paul tells the Corinthians in his exhortations on the legitimacy and necessity of marriage: "I wish all were as I myself am [i.e. celibate]. But each has a particular gift from God, one having one kind and another a different kind" (1 Cor 7:7). Paul prefers that everyone remain just as he or she is, for "the present form of this world is passing away" (7:31b), i.e. the final arrival of the end is imminent.

Thus, for both Jesus and Paul the question of celibacy has to do with the coming of the kingdom in the specific context of their respective ministries. Neither of them has in mind the development of the priesthood as we know it today. That development was greatly influenced by the fact that the end did not come and the church was faced with developing and refining her own internal structures. Once the church emerged from the severe persecution of the second and third centuries to becoming by 381 the established religion of the empire, monasticism with a corresponding idealization of virginity replaced martyrdom as the privileged form of witness, i.e. of being a dedicated Christian. During the first millennium there were both celibate (usually monks and religious) and married priests and bishops. The Orthodox churches still have both. Mandatory celibacy for all priests in the western Roman church was firmly established in the twelfth century. But, though tied to the priesthood, the church has always insisted that celibacy must be freely given and freely accepted. For priests today, their inspiration and motivation must be the same as that of Jesus and Paul: dedication to the ministry that the Lord has given to each one.

Q. 29. But wasn't Jesus himself a priest, or at least a rabbi? You seem to imply that the priesthood only started later.

Indeed, both the priesthood as Roman Catholics know it and the structured rabbinate as Orthodox Jews know it did develop after the time of Jesus. They both developed because of changed historical circumstances and needs. For both, a critical moment was the destruction of the temple in Jerusalem in 70 C.E. For Jews, the carrier of their traditions became the rabbis (heirs to the scribal and Pharisaic interpreters of the law at the time of Jesus). For Christians, the bishops became the carriers of tradition as the heirs to the apostolic and prophetic interpreters of the gospel after Jesus' death and resurrection.

As for Jesus, there is only one text in the entire NT that develops the notion of his priesthood, the letter to the Hebrews. Jesus is a priest forever according to the order of Melchizedek (i.e. of unknown and mysterious origins, but eternal: Heb 7:1–3) who has passed once and for all through the sanctuary by means of his death and exaltation to the right hand of God and so put an end to the levitical priesthood of the Old Testament (4:14–7:28). In effect, Jesus has offered the once-for-all sacrifice that has put an end to the need for more sacrifices and hence a continuing priesthood (8:1–10:39). "He entered once for all into the Holy Place, not with the blood of goats and calves, but with his own blood, thus obtaining eternal redemption" (9:12; see 9:25–26; 10:11–14). Thus, Christ is both priest and sacrificial victim who has brought to an end the need for any other. Christian priesthood must always understand itself as the sacramental embodiment of Christ's own priesthood, not as a new or different or even continuing priesthood. Christ is the only and unique high priest by reason of his death and resurrection.

Jesus during his historical ministry can in no sense be called a priest, i.e. he did not belong to the levitical priesthood of that time. Neither can he be called a rabbi in the later technical sense of one schooled in the law. However, he was called "teacher" (*rabbi*) in the generic sense of one who speaks words of wisdom. He was simply a Jewish layman, and indeed from an obscure and backward village called Nazareth. But, as such, he was a tremendous threat to the guardians of sacred power and authority, especially the priests and the temple aristocracy. Indeed, the chief priests, the scribes, and the elders ask him: "By what authority are you doing these things?" (Mk 11:28).

Q. 30. Why would the Jewish leaders ask that question if Jesus' authority came from God?

Once again, we know in the light of the resurrection that Jesus received "all authority in heaven and on earth" (Mt 28:18), but that was not so evident during his public ministry. Indeed, the great question between Jesus and his adversaries was whether he was right about God, this loving, all-inclusive and forgiving God that he was proclaiming. They accused him of blasphemy (Mk 2:6–7) and of casting out devils by the power of the devil (Mk 3:22). When finally asked about his authority, he responds with a question about the baptism of John, whether it came from heaven or was of human origin (Mk 11:27–33). The important point is that the question of Jesus' authority is related to John's baptism. This is where Mark begins his story of Jesus.

Mark, in a way parallel to the infancy narratives of Matthew and Luke, intends to convey the religious and theological conviction of Christian faith that Jesus' origins are of the Holy Spirit. The scene includes the heavenly revelation that he is the beloved Son of God. Hence, we have at the very beginning a vivid portrayal of Christian faith that includes Father, Son, and Spirit. Yet, underlying this is surely the historical fact that Jesus' ministry was a Spirit-filled ministry which began with the baptism of John. His healing power and his teaching authority are attributed to the presence and anointing of the Spirit. For example, when challenged about the origins of his healing power, he responds: "But if it is by the Spirit of God that I cast out demons, then the kingdom of God has come upon you" (Mt 12:28; Lk 11:20 has "finger" instead of "Spirit" but it conveys the same idea of God's power and authority). To the degree that his opponents do not discern the presence and power of the Spirit in his ministry here and now but rather speak against the Holy Spirit, they have a sin that does not admit of forgiveness for they have missed the critical and decisive moment of the kingdom's arrival (Mk 3:28–30; cp. Mt 12:32 = Lk 12:10). Luke has Jesus inaugurating his ministry at Nazareth by reading from Isaiah 61:1–2: "The Spirit of the Lord is upon me, because he has anointed me to bring good news to the poor . . ." (Lk 4:18; cp. Mt 11:2–6 par.). While the text is probably not historical as it stands, it does capture the historical reminiscence of Jesus' ministry of preaching, teaching, and healing as the works of one anointed by the power of the Spirit, a Spirit he received through the baptism of John.

Q. 31. If Jesus was the sinless Son of God from the moment of his conception, why did he need to be baptized?

The question you ask was already a problem by the time Matthew, Luke, and John were written and probably earlier. Undoubtedly, Mark's simple and straightforward presentation of Jesus' baptism is the historical reality: "In those days Jesus came from Nazareth of Galilee and was baptized by John in the Jordan" (Mk 1:9). Mark, as noted in the previous question, interprets that simple fact as a moment of divine revelation that includes the descent of the Spirit and the voice from heaven (the Father) who affirms that Jesus is "my beloved Son." To early Christians this would recall their own baptism "in the name of the Father and of the Son and of the Holy Spirit" (Mt 28:19) and so their complete identification with Jesus.

It is instructive to compare the treatment of Jesus' baptism in Matthew, Luke, and John. Such a comparison illustrates once again that an historical event like Jesus' baptism was taken up and reinterpreted according to the developing theological and religious interests of the early Christian communities. To summarize briefly: for Matthew (3:13–17), the baptism goes forward only after Jesus overcomes John's objections by saying that "it is proper for us in this way to fulfill all righteousness." This fits in with one of Matthew's central themes: that Jesus not only proclaims but also embodies in his whole life the will of God. Thus, Matthew's answer to your question is that Jesus, who is clearly the sinless Son of God from the moment of his conception, freely accepts baptism just as he will his death on the cross (cp. 26:42). For Luke, the issue is more complicated because John the Baptist belongs to the epoch of Israel as presented in the infancy narratives. Thus, he notes that Herod had shut John up in prison (3:19–20) before he narrates Jesus' baptism (vv. 21–22). Luke does not offer an explanation of the baptism itself. He only mentions it indirectly in order to focus on the revelation scene. However, his treatment reflects two of his central theological concerns: (1) Jesus as the one God anointed with the Holy Spirit and with power (Acts 10:38; Lk 4:16–21); (2) salvation history as clearly differentiated into the three epochs of Israel (Lk 1:5–3:20), of Jesus (Lk 3:21–24:53), and of the church (Acts). For John, as mentioned earlier (see Q. 14), both conception and baptism have been superseded by the understanding of Jesus as the Word in an eternal relation with the Father. John the Baptist can only be a witness to Jesus' transcendence. Thus, John does not have any account of Jesus' baptism.

The foregoing analysis gives historical credence to the simple fact that Jesus was baptized at the beginning of his public ministry. As such, it needed no further explanation. Jesus probably followed John for a time before he started out on his own. He may even have practiced baptism himself (Jn 3:22; cp. 4:1–2). In any event, Jesus' own baptism was undoubtedly the moment when he received his own mission from the Father in the power of the Spirit (see Q. 30).

Q. 32. What was that mission? What did the Father expect Jesus to do?

That is a good question, and not easy to answer. If we had only the gospel of John, we would think that he came to proclaim himself and his relation to the Father and the Spirit. In this sense, John's gospel represents the highly theological view of the early church. The synoptics offer a different view: he came not to proclaim himself but the fulfillment of the "time" and the nearness of the kingdom of God (Mk 1:15; Mt 4:17; Lk 4:21). He came in the manner of a prophet who announces "good news" to the people by calling them to confront the present crisis of oppression and humiliation. They will do this by remembering and retrieving what is deepest and best in their past. He was sent to his people Israel to offer them the true freedom of sons and daughters of God, to call them to their true vocation as a light to the Gentiles. By remembering God's true intention "from the beginning," the people are to respond with a radical change of mind and heart (repentance) that will allow God's truth to live in them here and now (faith) and so open up the possibility of the true future. This future will be created by God's initiative coupled with the people's responsiveness.

Jesus announced the approaching nearness of the kingdom of God in both word and deed, but its actual arrival depended on the people's response. This response should not be understood according to our western way of thinking, which is highly individualistic. This was a communal call and thus involved the transformation of social structures. For example, when Jesus said: "Blessed are you poor, for yours is the kingdom of God" (Lk 6:20; cp. Mt 5:3), he was not saying that it is a good thing to be poor. Neither was he saying that the poor are somehow more virtuous than the rich. He knew well enough that there are good people and evil people among rich and poor alike. But he was saying that God wants to change the situation of the poor, i.e. of those who are destitute and do not have the basic material necessities to be able to live a decent human life. This change cannot take place unless the structures that oppress and imprison them are changed. The kingdom can be said to have arrived when the captives are released, the blind see, and the oppressed go free (Lk 4:18).

Q. 33. Can you tell us more about what Jesus meant by "the kingdom of God"? Isn't that an outmoded concept for people who live in democratic societies?

Under the yoke of oppression, the common hopes and aspirations of the people in Jesus' day included at least the following: (1) only God is king over Israel, not Caesar; (2) God wants to free the people from their oppression (as celebrated every Passover recalling the exodus); (3) God will bring this about through some future event in history. This was expressed in images like the "Day of the Lord" and "God is King." Jesus chose a less current but still evocative image in "the kingdom of God." It was a symbol that called forth powerful expectations.

But Jesus gave it his own meaning. When asked by the Pharisees when the kingdom of God was coming, he answered: "The kingdom of God is not coming with things that can be observed; nor will they say, 'Look, here it is!' or 'There it is!' For, in fact, the kingdom of God is among you" (Lk 17:20–21). Here he seems to reject two popular forms of expectation. One, from the more educated scribal class, looked for some kind of divine intervention to destroy this present evil world and create a completely new one. This is an extreme form of apocalyptic, perhaps more common today than in Jesus' day, which looks for "signs" in the sky or in sacred texts in order to predict exactly when, where, and how the end will take place. In spite of many apocalyptic sects today that attempt to do just this, Jesus never tried to predict the future in this way. "But about that day or hour no one knows, neither the angels in heaven, nor the Son, but only the Father" (Mk 13:32). The other expectation came from the more popular level and looked for a warrior hero from the house of David who would overthrow the enemies of Israel and establish Israel as God's kingdom on earth. In its extreme form, this nationalistic hope would encourage rebellion through hatred of the enemy and their violent overthrow and destruction. Jesus clearly rejected such violent means to bring in the kingdom, for example when he said: "Do not resist an evildoer" (Mt 5:39) and "Love your enemies and pray for those who persecute you" (Mt 5:44).

These two popular forms of expectation look for some kind of divine intervention from outside to resolve the present crisis. Jesus, on the other hand, directs the attention within this world to the here and now realities that constitute human life. In effect he says: Do not look away from your human lives but more deeply into them in all the social, cultural, political, economic, and religious relationships that they involve. There you will discover the God of Israel alive, active, present. The symbol, kingdom of God, does not refer to a time or a place or a person other than ourselves. It refers rather to the God whom we seek in the midst of human life. That seems very "democratic," i.e. people-centered, to me.

Q. 34. If Jesus points to God at the center of human life, wasn't he just pointing to himself?

Ultimately, yes; mediately, no. What I mean by that is that the God revealed in Jesus finally includes Jesus himself. Full trinitarian faith is only possible in the light of the final and definitive revelation given in the resurrection, but that revelation was mediated to us through a human life, that of Jesus of Nazareth. Jesus' human life can be characterized as one empowered by the Spirit and intensely focused on the Father whom he called *Abba*. Thus, the final revelation of Father, Son, and Spirit is rooted and grounded in Jesus' human life and experience. This is the deeper dimension of everything he said and did.

Yet, Jesus did not come simply to convey information, whether about doctrine or about morals. He did not tell us what to believe or what to do, i.e. he did not give us a set of doctrines to be believed or moral rules to be followed. Like all great religious geniuses, he gave us rather a way of life which can only be understood through participation, i.e. the personal experience of following his way. That is why his teaching in parables was so important. He communicated what he meant by the kingdom of God in various ways, through proverbs and wisdom sayings, through healings and shared meals, but perhaps his favorite way was to tell stories, stories that did not allow people to be fence-sitters—like the children in the marketplace who refuse to participate fully in the game and then complain when things don't turn out right (Mt 11:16–17).

Q. 35. Could you say something more about parables? Doesn't this way of teaching just serve to confuse people?

Parables are not intended to confuse but they are intended to confound, i.e. to get us thinking and reflecting about the comfortable and ordered world we thought we knew. A normal reaction to a parable would be: I think I know what you mean by that, but I know I don't like it. Parables are stories that demand participation. They do not just inform us about aspects of the kingdom or illustrate ideas we already have about God or human morals. The parables *are* the reality of the kingdom. Jesus talks about the ordinary, everyday lived experience of his contemporaries: a woman making bread, a sower sowing seed, a traveler beset by robbers, a younger son leaving for foreign lands, laborers needing work, etc. Yet the stories are exaggerated, the familiar becomes unfamiliar, the ordinary extraordinary. This *is* the reality of the kingdom for those who have eyes to see and ears to hear (Mk 4:9.23). The kingdom of God is precisely *there,* in the midst of human life (Lk 17:21), not in some other world that would alienate us from our concretely lived experience here and now.

To illustrate: the parable we call the "prodigal son" (Lk 15:11–32) can legitimately be used as an allegory in which the key lies outside the parable. So the correct interpretation of the parable depends on our already knowing that the father is God, the younger son is repentant Israel, and the elder son is unrepentant Israel. Luke intends it this way with his theme of joy in heaven over one sinner who repents (Lk 15:1–2.7.10.17–19.32). Luke has conditioned us to read the parable this way and rightly so, for his perspective is that of Christian faith in the risen Lord. The point is that this is a legitimate reading in the changed historical circumstances of the early church, but we can still ask what it might have meant for Jesus in his historical situation.

It seems to me that if we take the story on its own terms as a story about the limitations and possibilities of human behavior, then it is simply a story about how fathers treat sons and sons treat fathers, as well as a story about how brothers treat one another. Thus, it is a story about real people with real problems. I think Jesus is saying that if we would enter into the kingdom of God, then we must enter ever more deeply into that most fundamental of human relationships, that of parent-child. We must heal what needs to be healed and express the kind of unconditional and transforming love that this father had for his two sons. If we can see and hear this new possibility for ourselves, then we will discover the God of Jesus alive, active, present at the very center of such relationships. Jesus in his parabolic teaching seeks the transformation of human relationships on all levels of society.

Q. 36. Didn't Jesus speak more directly about God? What does *Abba* mean for him?

Jesus called people to discover the God of Israel alive, active, present in the midst of human life. But surely the one who is to be discovered at the deepest center of our lives is the God he called *Abba*. *Abba* is a Hebrew or Aramaic word used as such only once in the gospels when Jesus is praying in the garden of Gethsemane: "Abba, Father, for you all things are possible, remove this cup from me; yet, not what I want but what you want" (Mk 14:36). Only Mark gives us the actual word and he also gives us the correct translation: *Father!* (*ho pater*). It is a vocative form used in an emphatic way, thus appropriate for prayer. In the only other instances where the original word actually occurs, Paul twice recalls its import as a prayer (probably with the Gethsemane tradition in mind). He says, in effect, if you want a sign that you are truly a child of God in the

Son (and so an heir to Christ), it is the ability given you by the Spirit to pray "Abba! Father!" (Gal 4:6; Rom 8:15–16). In such prayer we find the experiential basis of our trinitarian faith.

As far as we know, no one before Jesus had ever prayed to God with the word *Abba*. It is a colloquial and familiar word, a word a child might use, but it is not a childish word. It connotes a depth of familiarity and intimacy that would stay with a child throughout his or her adult life. Thus it is not a word just for children but for anyone who experiences such a relationship of trust, closeness, and respect for a father or a revered teacher. Jesus uses it in a critical moment of great agony and fear to speak with the one who has been the center of his whole life, the God whom he knew as a gracious and loving Father, the one who feeds the birds of the air and clothes the lilies of the field, who counts the very hairs on our heads and knows how to give us good things.

I would add that the important thing about the image is not its masculinity. Indeed, unlike the dominance of a patriarchal father, this is an *Abba* who feeds and clothes us, who cares for us and nurtures us, who embraces us with the kind of total and unconditional love that the father had for his two sons in the parable. This is a God of compassionate understanding and forgiveness, a God who reaches out to embrace the poor, the despised, the marginalized, the outcast. This is the God of Jesus proclaimed by him in both word and deed, a God who could be called "Mother!" as well as "Father!"

Q. 37. If Jesus was really God, why did he need to pray as he did in the garden?

Your question underlines a recurring theme. We frequently think of Jesus' divinity as so overpowering or controlling that his humanity becomes very secondary and unimportant. This is the influence of later tradition that has emphasized the divinity. It begins with the gospel of John, e.g. Jesus' prayer in John 17 is spoken by one who knows all things and is now returning to the eternal glory which he had with the Father before the foundation of the world (Jn 17:5). Earlier prayers in John are the same. Jesus thanks the Father for hearing him, but then offers the qualification: "I knew that you always hear me, but I have said this for the sake of the crowd standing here, so that they may believe that you sent me" (Jn 11:42; cp. 12:27–28, which is John's version of the agony in the garden). This is probably our normal image of Jesus at prayer. John certainly captures what is central and decisive in the historical life of Jesus: his personal relation to the Father.

But the synoptics present a different perspective from that of John, one that emphasizes the human struggles and temptations of Jesus. Here prayer, not simply as eternal conversation with the Father but as expressing the joys and anxieties of our human condition, seems normal and necessary. Jesus is said to have spent hours, even whole nights, in solitary prayer (Mk 1:35; 6:46 par.; Lk 5:16; 6:12; 9:18.28; 11:1; 22:41–46—obviously Luke emphasizes the image of Jesus at prayer). There are very few recorded prayers of Jesus, but the ones we have, while influenced by the religious and theological interests of the early church, are certainly historical in this: that they express Jesus' absolute trust in the love and fidelity of his *Abba,* particularly in the face of what would appear to contradict such trust. He thanks the Father for his wisdom in the face of the conflict and failure he was experiencing in his ministry (Mt 11:25; Lk 10:21 places the same prayer in a context of joy over the success of the seventy-two disciples). He affirms the Father's will in the midst of his agony and fear (Mk 14:36 par.). On the cross, he invokes Psalm 22, a psalm of trust in the face of God's seeming abandonment (Mk 15:34 = Mt 27:46; Lk 23:34.46 replaces this prayer with two prayers for forgiveness and for complete trust in the Father). However historical any of these prayers may be individually, they are all (including John) historical in this: they express the intensity and concentratedness of Jesus' relation to the Father and his complete and total trust in the Father's will. We all need such prayer as we face the struggles, ambiguities, and uncertainties of human life.

Q. 38. What about temptations? Would Jesus have experienced temptations as we do?

The question of temptation and sin is, it seems to me, the touchstone of how seriously we take Jesus' humanity. Did he really experience everything we experience? The letter to the Hebrews thinks so. Although it has a clear doctrine of Jesus' divinity expressed as God's Wisdom exalted to the right hand of Majesty on high (1:1–4) and so superior to the prophets, to the angels, to Moses, to the priests and temple sacrifices, it can also say: ". . . we do not have a high priest who is unable to sympathize with our weaknesses, but we have one who in every respect has been tested as we are, yet without sin" (4:15). The word translated as "tested" also means "tempted." And again: "Although he was Son, he learned obedience through what he suffered" (5:8), said in reference to his prayer in the garden.

Whatever we say about Jesus' divinity, we must allow his humanity to come into full play. We know that he did not sin, not because we can analyze the interior states of his mind, but because God raised him from the dead. But the fact that he had to "learn obedience" implies human struggle against the forces of evil. Obedience is a matter of human will, not divine will. Paul portrays Jesus' human life as reversing the disobedience of Adam through his own obedience (Rom 5:12–21). This means that Jesus entered fully into the struggles and weaknesses of human life dominated by the powers of sin, law, and death, and *there,* from within as it were, transformed human disobedience. Paul speaks of God sending his own Son "in the likeness of sinful flesh" (Rom 8:3), which is to say with Hebrews that he was like us in all things except sin (cp. Phil 2:6–8). His need to learn obedience, his struggle to remain faithful to the Father's will even unto death, was for these authors real.

The synoptic narratives of the temptations, especially as developed in Matthew and Luke, are compressed theological accounts of what probably took place throughout the ministry of Jesus. They touch the central concern of his mission, which was to renew Israel, by recalling Israel's own temptations: to prefer God's miraculous gifts (manna) to God's will; to tempt God to prove God's care and benevolence; and finally to replace the worship of God with the worship of idols. Jesus, like Israel, had to remain faithful to God's will and to trust in God's care and benevolence, not demand proof of it. He had to work out the true meaning of the mission the Father had given him, especially when those around him had other ideas: "When Jesus realized that they were about to come and take him by force to make him king, he withdrew again to the mountain by himself" (Jn 6:15).

Q. 39. Wasn't Jesus a king? I have heard some people say he was a revolutionary and that he wanted to overthrow the ruling powers with violence. Is that true?

When Pilate asks Jesus, "Are you the King of the Jews?" (Mk 15:2 par.), all four gospels note that Jesus' response is non-committal. It is Pilate who says so. This implies two things historically. First, the Romans crucified him on the only grounds that they could understand, namely that he was a rebel who was stirring up the people and challenging the authority of the emperor by calling himself a king (Lk 23:1–5). This would not be unusual as there were other rebel kings who had tried to do the same during Rome's occupation of Palestine. The inscription on the cross: "The King of the Jews" (Mk 15:26) should thus be seen as a mockery of Jewish pretensions. The appropriate title would have been "King of Israel," and there is great irony in Mark when the chief priests and scribes mock him but use the correct titles: "Let the Messiah, the King of Israel, come down from the cross now, so that we may see and believe" (Mk 15:32).

The second historical implication is that Jesus himself rejected both titles, i.e. Messiah and King, precisely because of their nationalistic implications. Jesus was indeed revolutionary in the sense of calling for a radical transformation of society, but he was not a "revolutionist" in the sense of advocating the violent overthrow of the enemies of Israel. He chose another way, that of compassionate love and forgiveness extending even to enemies. He rejected the principle of retaliation, "an eye for an eye and a tooth for a tooth," even though this principle was meant to limit and control the amount and kind of revenge one could take. Instead he says: "Do not resist the evildoer" (Mt 5:39). He is not saying: Do not resist evil. Jesus obviously resisted evil in his life. But he is saying: Do not resist evil with evil but with good. Turning the other cheek, giving your clothes to one who demands them, going the extra mile is not to say that insults, robbery, and forced labor are good. It is to say that the only way to overcome evil is to transform the evil through what is good and loving rather than to increase the evil. Paul says the same thing in Romans 12:14–21 where he concludes: ". . . by doing this you will heap burning coals on their heads," i.e. touch their consciences and perhaps bring them to a true conversion of mind and heart.

When we today celebrate the feast of Christ the King we should remember that he was crucified by the imperial powers according to their understanding of what these titles meant. His victory in the resurrection is a triumph over just such powers with their crushing violence. On the cross Jesus transformed the meaning of both Christ and King.

Q. 40. But what about Satan? Wasn't Jesus' victory over the power of the devil?

Indeed it was. This is the way Mark 1:12–13 presents the temptation of Jesus. The conflict is between the Spirit who literally "casts him out into the desert" and Satan who tempts him for forty days. The messianic victory is signaled by two observations. First, "he was with the wild beasts," i.e. he was restoring the harmony between humans and nature like the young child in Isaiah 11:6–9 who leads the animals and plays with them. Second, "the angels served him at table," i.e. he was celebrating the messianic feast that unites heaven and earth. A similar triad occurs in Luke 10:18–20 when the disciples return to tell him that even the demons submit to them: (1) Satan falling like lightning; (2) authority to tread on snakes and scorpions; (3) names written in heaven. There is no doubt that the gospels present Jesus as ultimately battling the power of Satan. The early church recognized that "our struggle is not against enemies of blood and flesh, but against the rulers, against the authorities, against the cosmic powers of this present darkness, against the spiritual forces of evil in the heavenly places" (Eph 6:12; cp. Rom 8:38; 1 Cor 15:24–26).

Luke sees Satan's influence primarily during the temptations and again at the cross when "Satan entered into Judas" (22:3 anticipated at 4:13). But there seems to be no doubt that Jesus himself saw the many manifestations of evil arrayed against him, especially the myriad demon possessions and the hostility of the Jewish leadership, as symbolically one evil force that he called "Satan." He asks, when accused of casting out demons by the ruler of demons, "How can Satan cast out Satan?" (Mk 3:23). For Jesus to be successful, he must first bind the strong man (3:27). Those who accuse him of having an unclean spirit have blasphemed against the Holy Spirit and can never have forgiveness (3:28–30).

However one imagines the devil, as a personal angelic being or not, the struggle is against the power of evil that is real and much more pervasive and systemic than the powers of any single individual. Yet this does not excuse anyone from personal responsibility. In Mark, Jesus is presented as one mighty in word and work. He has coercive power over demons, over illnesses, over nature, but not over the human heart. The great obstacle to his mission was "hardness of heart" on the part of the leaders (3:5–6), of his own people at Nazareth (6:1–6), and even, perhaps especially in Mark, of his disciples (6:52; 8:14–21). Neither Jesus nor Satan can force human beings to respond if they refuse.

Q. 41. Why did Jesus put up with all the bad treatment he got from so many people during his lifetime? After all, he was the Son of God!

The centurion at the foot of the cross, seeing how he died, exclaims: "Truly this man was God's Son!" (Mk 15:39). For Mark, what it means to call Jesus "Christ" or "Son of God" or "Son of Man" can only be understood when we stand at the foot of the cross and experience for ourselves how he died. The answer to his question "Who do you say that I am?" (8:29) is not Peter's confession of faith but his acceptance of the cross as something personally experienced. Jesus came as "this man," the Son of Man who "came not to be served but to serve" (10:45), the servant who "will not break a bruised reed or quench a smoldering wick until he brings justice to victory" (Mt 12:20, citing the servant song of Is 42:1–4).

Jesus' very life and death is the revelation of God, a God who does not intervene to force people to do the divine will but rather invites them to be free children of God, free as Jesus was free. Jesus was free to confront the power of evil and hypocrisy that surrounded him. He was free to call others to follow him on his way and to share his homelessness and insecurity. He was free to trust utterly and totally in the goodness of his Father even when everything seemed to contradict such trust. He was free to love and embrace the rejected and despised, including women and children, and to call that God's will, God's justice. He was free to put up with all the bad treatment he got precisely because he was God's Son, and like his Father his way was the way of compassion, forgiveness, and inclusive love. Any other way would break the reed and snuff out the wick. It would not bring the freedom for which Christ has set us free (Gal 5:1).

Q. 42. There's so much suffering in the world, both then and now. Did Jesus really have the power to heal?

There is no question in my mind that Jesus cured people possessed by demons or suffering from illnesses. It is important to note that his ministry of healing was intended to restore people not only physically but morally and spiritually as well, i.e. to heal the whole person and reintegrate that person into society. Jesus' miracles were intended also to announce the arrival of the kingdom: "If it is by the Spirit of God that I cast out demons, then the kingdom of God has come upon you" (Mt 12:28 par.).

The gospels, especially Mark, portray Jesus as very much involved in the suffering of the sick and personally affected by the process of healing. He not only reaches out to empower the sick by his healing touch but is himself empowered to heal by their faith. Indeed, Matthew makes explicit the connection between the power of faith and the power to heal in Jesus' ministry (Mt 13:58; cp. Mk 6:5–6). To me, one of the most moving accounts is the story of the woman who had been suffering from hemorrhages for twelve years (Mk 5:25–34). In such a condition, she should not even appear in public, much less come up to a man in a crowd and touch him! One can only imagine the courage it took for her to overcome her fear and break the taboo. But Jesus pushes the point. He knows that power had gone forth from him and insists: "Who touched my clothes?" When the woman in fear and trembling steps forth and tells him the whole truth, he says to her: "Daughter, your faith has made you well. . . ." He attributes the healing neither to God nor to himself, but to the power of her faith, i.e. of her ability to overcome her fear of oppressive structures and to reach out in her need, trusting in another to help her. Her healing has also restored her to the community as a daughter of Abraham (cp. Lk 13:16).

The same point is made in the story of Jairus' daughter that is intertwined with this one (Mk 5:21–24.35–43). Both her age (twelve) and her death would mark her as unclean. Yet, Jesus tells Jairus not to fear, only to have faith. When he takes her by the hand and raises her up, he tells them to give her something to eat—a curious detail were it not for the fact that she too is now restored to the community symbolized by the sharing of meals. Two women, considered unclean, experiencing the mutual empowerment of faith, touching or being touched by Jesus at a moment of symbolic fulfillment (the number twelve), restored to full participation in the community: this is the kind of wholeness that Jesus' healing ministry was intended to create.

Q. 43. How much power did Jesus have? Could he do anything?

Jesus certainly was an exorcist who cast out demons from possessed people, and he was a healer who sought to make people whole on the physical, moral, and spiritual level. As already suggested, he was empowered to heal by the faith of those involved, whether of the person who was sick or of a friend or a relative who interceded for the sick person. But he was also empowered by the Spirit who anointed him at his baptism so that ". . . the blind receive their sight, the lame walk, the lepers are cleansed, the deaf hear, the dead are raised, and the poor have good news brought to them" (Mt 11:5 par., referring to Is 29:18–19; 35:5–6; 61:1; cp. Lk 4:18–19). This is said in response to John the Baptist's question: "Are you the one who is to come or are we to wait for another?" (Mt 11:3 par.).

Jesus' healing ministry is primarily intended to be a powerful symbol of the arrival of the kingdom of God (Mt 12:28 par.) and should be understood in this context. Thus, his power comes from the one who anointed him (the Spirit) and from the one who sent him on his mission (the Father). It is not a power to do anything whatsoever. It is a power given to restore and renew Israel. Jesus' healing ministry strikingly embodies and evokes the remembrance of Israel *past:* poor and oppressed under the yoke of Egypt, blind and deaf, lame and even dead. His healing ministry celebrates Israel *present,* the Israel whose God is the God of Abraham, Isaac, and Jacob, i.e. a God "not of the dead but of the living" (Mk 12:27 par.). His healing ministry evokes hope for Israel *future,* an Israel whose memory is imaginatively creative of a world in which there are no more poor, despised, and marginated ones in her midst. His power is meant to empower others so that they too might go forth, like the twelve who symbolize a renewed Israel, "to proclaim the message and to have authority to cast out demons" (Mk 3:14c–15 par.; cp. Mk 6:7–13 par.). Thus, his power is not his alone but is for all to whom it is given.

From this perspective, we should lay to rest once and for all any notion of Jesus as some kind of super-hero who could do anything he wanted and who was the most handsome, intelligent, athletic, etc. of anyone who has ever lived. He was a man like us. He lived an ordinary and seemingly uneventful life until about the age of thirty when he was empowered by the Spirit of God for his mission. Once again, whatever we say of his divinity, it should not negate or ignore the full reality of his humanness. Luke offers a telling summary of Jesus' ministry: ". . . how God anointed Jesus of Nazareth with the Holy Spirit and with power; how he went about doing good and healing all who were oppressed by the devil, for God was with him" (Acts 10:38).

Q. 44. But what about Jesus' power over nature? Did he really walk on water and feed five thousand people at one time?

The so-called "nature miracles" present a different kind of question. While one may be able to understand the possibility of healing various kinds of sicknesses, even demon possession, within the normal processes of human illness and health, it is much more difficult to understand interventions that seem to reverse the normal processes of nature. One might well ask: What would be the point of such interventions? The danger with nature miracles is that they appeal to our desire for the phenomenal, for the miraculous for its own sake. Such stories can take on a kind of circus atmosphere.

In the gospels, there are three raisings of the dead (the young girl at Mk 5:35–43 par.; the widow's son at Lk 7:11–17; and Lazarus at Jn 11:1–44) and seven nature miracles (calming the storm at Mk 4:35–41 par.; walking on water at Mk 6:45–52 par.; feeding in the wilderness at Mk 6:34–44 par. and at Mk 8:1–9 par.; cursing the fig tree at Mk 11:12–14.20 par.; the coin in the fish's mouth at Mt 17:24–27; Peter's great catch of fish at Lk 5:1–11; cp. Jn 21:3–13; and the turning of water into wine at Jn 2:1–11). Although each must be analyzed separately, one can say in general that all of these stories are more concerned about Christian faith in the risen Lord than about any actual historical events that may or may not have happened. As mentioned earlier (Q. 4), the rather odd empirical fact of Jesus contravening the laws of nature by calming a storm or walking on water is not the really important point at issue. Rather, it is whether we experience him as risen Lord today helping us confront and overcome the fears and anxieties in our own hearts.

To take the example of the feedings in the wilderness, there is obvious symbolism in feeding five thousand and then later four thousand as representing Jesus' outreach to the Jewish and Gentile worlds respectively. Each gospel (including Jn 6:1–14) records the feeding of the five thousand, but only Mark and Matthew repeat the story of the four thousand. Obviously, the story has great theological importance. A detail often overlooked (and not in John's account) is key to understanding the story. Jesus' first response to the disciples is: "You give them something to eat." And when, following their objections, he does multiply the five loaves and two fish, he first gives them to the disciples so that *they* distribute the food among the people. Whether Jesus ever actually performed such a phenomenal feat, does not the miracle happen everytime we share our food with the hungry? Everytime we take bread and fish or whatever we have, bless, break, and distribute to all present, does not the miracle happen? Is this not the most fundamental meaning of communion?

Q. 45. What happened at the last supper? Did Jesus really change bread and wine into his body and blood? Isn't that a nature miracle?

This is another instance where it is important to distinguish an historical question from a theological one. It seems very probable historically that Jesus did share a final meal with his disciples as he faced the very real probability of his meeting a violent death. But it is impossible from the viewpoint of historical method to know what actually happened because all the accounts as we have them (1 Cor 11:23–26; Mk 14:22–25 par.; Jn 13:1ff; 6:35–50 and 51–58) are primarily concerned with communicating the significance of his death on the cross. Paul sees the eating and drinking as a proclamation of the Lord's death until he comes. He is clearly recalling the eucharistic practice of the Christian communities, as are the synoptics. Paul and the synoptics, all in slightly different ways, view the body and blood as representing the sacrificial offering of Jesus on the cross for the sake of others, i.e. for our salvation.

John, on the other hand, has no words of institution corresponding to the other four authors. However, Jesus' insistence on washing the feet of Peter is intended to bring out the importance and necessity of the cross if Peter is to have any part with him in the future. The following discourses in John (chapters 13–17) all focus on Jesus' going to the Father, i.e. the necessity of his death. The earlier bread of life discourse (6:35–50) concludes with the exhortation (vv. 51–58) to eat his flesh and drink his blood in order to live forever. Clearly, all of these accounts reflect the early church's faith in the crucified and risen Lord as experienced now in their eucharistic practice.

When we pronounce these same words of institution at mass, we are celebrating in a sacramental way the power and presence of the risen Lord. Does the bread and wine change? The church has always maintained that, on the level of what we normally consider bread and wine to be, it remains the same, i.e. physical appearance, color, shape, taste, etc. The mystery is that it is no longer simply bread and wine because it has been transformed into the real presence of the risen Lord. However one wishes to explain it on a philosophical level, the bread and wine now embody sacramentally the reality of Jesus' presence in a way that is unique and that does not allow us to consider this bread and wine as simply bread and wine. This is a miracle but it does not contravene the laws of nature. Rather, the eucharist celebrates and embodies in a deeper way the presence of the risen Lord who is already present in the celebrating community by reason of faith and baptism.

Q. 46. The gospels seem to present Jesus as angry and frustrated at times, e.g. why would he insult that foreign woman, calling her a dog and refusing to heal her daughter, or why would he curse a fig tree and kill it?

If Jesus was fully human, then of course he experienced the full range of human emotions, not only anger and frustration, but fear, anxiety, hope, love, fidelity. Anger, like guilt, is a good and healthy emotion if there is a justified reason for it. Mark presents the reality and depth of Jesus' feelings more straightforwardly than the other gospels and thus gives us a more human picture of him. A good example of anger is his reaction to the silent hypocrisy and hardness of heart of his accusers: "He looked around at them with anger" (Mk 3:5; Matthew and Luke in the parallels omit any reference to his anger and grief). His frustration seems clear when he asks his obtuse disciples: "Why are you talking about having no bread? Do you still not perceive or understand? Are your hearts hardened?" (Mk 8:17; parallel in Matthew but not in Luke).

The two examples referred to in the question again illustrate the difference between a healing miracle and a nature miracle. The story of the Syrophoenician woman (Mk 7:24–30) who in Matthew (15:21–28) is a Canaanite woman, in either case a foreigner outside Israel, is remarkable for the persistence of this woman who will not take "no" for an answer, not even from Jesus! Her whole being is concentrated on the one thing that concerns her, the health of her daughter, and she will endure any insult and degradation to have her daughter restored to her. Jesus indeed insults her: "Let the children be fed first, for it is not fair to take the children's food and throw it to the dogs." But she has a ready answer: "Sir, even the dogs under the table eat the children's crumbs." It is a remarkable story of faith, as Matthew notes: "Woman, great is your faith!" Jesus is not only empowered to heal because of her faith; he also learns from her that such power is intended also for the lost sheep outside the house of Israel (Mt 15:24).

The cursing of the fig tree (Mk 11:12–14.20 = Mt 21:18–19; cp. Lk 13:6–9) is the occasion for an exhortation to have faith in God, probably in contrast to Israel (symbolized by the fig tree) which did not know the time of her visitation and so bears no fruit. In other words, it is another story from the perspective of the resurrection faith of the early community, using nature to illustrate the contrast between Jesus' rejection during his historical ministry and his acceptance after his death by those who believe in him. This faith gives to Christians the power to move mountains. Nothing will be impossible to the Christian who has faith and prays (Mk 11:21–24 par.).

Q. 47. Was Jesus always forgiving and loving, non-violent and peaceful?

As already suggested, Jesus was a man of strong emotions. In reference to the question, I would suggest three virtues (while not excluding others) which have strong emotional overtones. He was a man of decisiveness, compassion, and fidelity. Matthew 23:23, in a passage characteristic of his theology, speaks of "the weightier matters of the law": justice (*krisis*), mercy (*eleos*), and faith (*pistis*). I am translating these as decisiveness, compassion, and fidelity.

First, Jesus was a man of decisiveness. He was given a mission, and in the manner of the prophets before him that mission included confrontation with the injustice and hypocrisy of his time. He was not afraid to call a spade a spade and condemn the deviousness and self-justifications of the "righteous." He came to call "sinners" (Mk 2:17 par.), i.e. those who could recognize and accept their need for God's gracious love and forgiveness. Moreover, he was not afraid to enter the temple and purify it of the buyers and sellers so that it would truly be "a house of prayer for all the nations" (Mk 11:17). In a word, his non-violence and peace could only make sense if he was a strong advocate for justice, not an apathetic and meek bystander.

Second, he was a man of compassion. It is a word used frequently of Jesus in his healing ministry, and it is used by Jesus, in his two best parables, of the Samaritan (Lk 10:33) and of the father who sees his younger son returning (Lk 15:20). It does not mean a mere sentiment of pity (as it is often translated) but rather such an identification with the suffering of another that the suffering becomes one's own and moves one to do whatever is possible to alleviate the suffering. Compassion moves one to action. Jesus sought a deep transformation of his society that would forever put an end to the misery of the poor, the sick, the possessed, and the excluded.

Finally, he was a man of fidelity. Unfortunately, a Greek word used only in Matthew (*praũs*) has usually been translated as "meek" and has given us a picture of Jesus as mild and passive in the face of conflict. Nothing could be further from the truth! For Matthew, Jesus not only teaches God's word or will; he embodies it in faithful obedience. He lives the will of his Father even unto death. Thus, the beatitude should be translated: "Blessed are those who faithfully do the will of God" (Mt 5:6), for the same word (*praũs*) is applied to Jesus as God's Wisdom from whom we should learn (11:29: ". . . for I am obedient and lowly in heart") and as the obedient king who enters Jerusalem to face death (21:5). In this, as in the other virtues, Jesus should be seen as a man courageous in his convictions and strong in love.

Q. 48. Sometimes Jesus seems too serious. Did he ever lighten up and show a sense of humor?

Our sources are so heavily focused on the cross that it can appear at times as if Jesus lived nothing but a miserable life. Joy only comes after his resurrection. This, of course, is a false perception. Jesus was a man of joy who deeply understood the foibles of human life and the graciousness of a loving God.

His sayings and parables manifest a creative poetic imagination. He had an eye for making the seemingly insignificant details of ordinary life extraordinary. He had a loving and sympathetic understanding of the human predicament. He loved irony and riddles, e.g. "The first will be last and the last will be first." His parables were intended, often in a humorous way, to upset the comfortable and ordered world of those in charge of "correct" interpretation of the law. What does it mean to say that the kingdom of God is a woman who took leaven and hid it in three measures of flour until it was all leavened (Mt 13:33 par.)? What does a *woman,* who is not a public figure and should have nothing to do with the serious matter of the kingdom, or *leaven,* which is a symbol of corruption, or *hiding,* have to do with the kingdom of God? Or even the huge amount of bread that results?

Jesus did not simply proclaim the kingdom in his teaching; he celebrated it with a joyous and seemingly at times raucous table-fellowship so that he is accused of being "a glutton and a drunkard, a friend of tax-collectors and sinners" (Mt 11:19 par.). He is challenged for not fasting and can only reply: Can the wedding guests fast while the wedding is going on? (Mk 2:18–22 par.). He loved wedding feasts and large banquets and saw them as images of God's kingdom. It was particularly offensive to his adversaries that he celebrated such feasts with "tax-collectors and sinners" (Mk 2:15–17 par.; Lk 15:1–2), i.e. with those who were looked upon as outside the law and so reprobate. Jesus not only told such as these that they too belonged to the kingdom; by breaking bread and sharing wine with them he was actually including them in the blessing of the kingdom as experienced here and now. Everyone was invited. Those who refused to come for reasons of purity and holiness excluded themselves. Jesus' sense of humor is nowhere more touchingly evident than in the story of Zacchaeus, this rich but despised tax-collector who was too short to see Jesus in the crowd and so ran ahead and climbed a sycamore tree. "Zacchaeus, hurry and come down; for I must stay at your house today." And they all grumbled because he went to be a guest in the house of a sinner (Lk 19:1–10).

Q. 49. Could you say something about forgiveness? Why would Jesus call "sinners" but not the "righteous"?

Forgiveness demands a recognition of one's need for forgiveness and a willing acceptance of one's dependence on another for forgiveness to happen. We find it hard both to forgive and to be forgiven because the very act breaks down our image as independent and self-made. When Jesus says that he came to call not the righteous but sinners, I take the term "righteous" to mean the self-righteous, i.e. those who consider themselves justified by their own actions. In the parable of the Pharisee and the tax-collector praying in the temple (Lk 18:10–13), Luke understands it this way (vv. 9.14). Yet it is not just a question of which one is justified. In a sense, both are justified: the Pharisee by observance of the law, the tax-collector by his humble plea for mercy. What is not justified is the Pharisee's attitude toward the tax-collector. He looks upon him and other sinners with contempt and considers them already excluded from God's mercy. It is the hardness of heart that excludes others from God's mercy and forgiveness that Jesus challenged by his out-reach to and inclusion of "tax-collectors and sinners" in the kingdom. The attitude of the tax-collector in the parable represents the necessary recognition of one's need and acceptance of one's dependence in order to enter the kingdom of God. Unlike the Pharisee, the tax-collector does not make invidious comparisons. Jesus offers an uncompromising challenge when he says: "Truly I tell you, the tax-collectors and the prostitutes are going into the kingdom of God ahead of you" (Mt 21:31).

God's forgiveness cannot take place, i.e. be effective, except and to the degree that we actually forgive one another (Mt 6:14–15). I understand the petition for forgiveness in the Lord's Prayer, as Matthew's wording has it (Mt 6:12), to mean that God's forgiveness is always already in action. God, who is love, is always offering the divine forgiveness. But God's forgiveness cannot be truly effective in human life if human beings harden their hearts toward others and refuse to forgive them. God's forgiveness, as God's love, empowers us to forgive and love one another, but it is only in the actual moment of forgiving and loving others that we experience God's forgiveness and love in the midst of our lives. Behind the petition for bread, which parallels the petition for forgiveness in the Lord's Prayer, is surely Jesus' practice of table-fellowship with tax-collectors and sinners. Breaking bread and sharing wine with Jesus at table was an experience of forgiveness and divine blessing, a truly liberating experience of the kingdom of God which is "in your midst" (Lk 17:21).

Q. 50. If Jesus was so inclusive and invited everyone into the kingdom, why did he exclude women from the priesthood?

We have already suggested (Q. 29) that the priesthood as we know it developed after the life and death of Jesus. Hence, it is futile to attribute attitudes or intentions to him with regard to the specific question of women priests that preoccupies us today. But it is worth saying something about his attitude toward and treatment of women during his historical ministry, for such knowledge can serve to challenge and correct attitudes that are prejudicial toward or demeaning of women.

In Jesus' day, women, along with children, slaves, and animals, were subject to the patriarchal authority of the male head of the family. They had no rights independently of their husbands. They could not divorce. Their place was in the home and, if in a public place, they were to keep silent, especially with strangers, and to go about their business unnoticed. They were not educated in the law and certainly were not to enter into the all-male discussions of a teacher and his disciples.

Jesus showed remarkable freedom in breaking all of these taboos. He engaged women in conversation in public (e.g. Jn 4:5–42; note the disciples' reaction of astonishment that he was speaking with a woman). He healed them, touching them and being touched by them in public (see Q. 42). Particularly notable is the story of "the woman who was a sinner" (Lk 7:36–50). Simon the Pharisee's shocked reaction to the woman's presence and actions would speak for many: ". . . who and what kind of woman this is who is touching him . . ." For Jesus, this was a moment of healing made possible by a woman's faith. He praised women for their faith (Mk 12:41–44 par.; Mt 15:28) and saw them as images of God's kingdom (Lk 15:8–10; Mt 13:33 par.; 23:37 par.). Most importantly, he called them to be with him on the way (Lk 8:1–3) and he defended their right to be disciples and sit among the male disciples as equals to hear his teaching. The story of Martha and Mary (Lk 10:38–42) is about two women, one who chooses to be about her tasks in the home and the other who chooses to sit at Jesus' feet as a disciple. Jesus defends Mary who "has chosen the better part, which will not be taken from her." Nor was it, for all the gospels record that the revelation that Jesus of Nazareth was raised from the dead was first given to his women disciples who then announced it to the male disciples. If, according to Paul, an apostle is one who has seen the risen Lord and so is the very foundation of the church (1 Cor 9:1–2), it would seem that women as well as men could be called apostles at the time of the church's origins.

Q. 51. When did the church start? I thought Jesus founded the church we have today.

The church we have today is the product of two thousand years of history. She is in continuity with the traditions of the past but, as a living embodiment of those traditions through the ages, she has adapted and transformed herself under the guidance of the Holy Spirit. Yet her foundational mission given to her from apostolic times has always been the same: to proclaim the good news that God has raised Jesus from the dead, to embody that good news in her own internal relationships of community and sacrament, and to serve the world in which she lives by transforming personal relationships and social structures through gospel values discerned in the Spirit. Thus, the church as we know it was born in the resurrection experience. She lives in the presence of the risen Lord, who is with her always to the end of time (Mt 28:20).

Yet this church is called a "community of disciples." She would not be the church of Jesus Christ if she were not rooted and grounded in Jesus of Nazareth. Thus, while Jesus during his historical ministry did not formally found the church as we know it, much less lay out a kind of blueprint regarding the future shape of governance or sacramental life, his proclamation of the kingdom, his way of life, his concerns for personal and social transformation are integral to Christian self-understanding. Jesus' mission was "to the lost sheep of the house of Israel" (Mt 15:24). He called the twelve as a symbol of a renewed Israel. He traveled among the villages and towns of his own people, seeking to bring into their hearts that profound transformation that would renew and revitalize Israel and so realize her true vocation as a light to the Gentiles.

I think we must recognize that he failed, that his mission from the Father ended in rejection, defeat, and death. The resurrection signals a new birth, a new beginning, indeed a new creation (2 Cor 5:17; Gal 6:15), both for him and for those who belong to him in resurrection faith. The post-resurrection church gradually came to understand herself not only as the true fulfillment of the promises given to Israel, which promises remain according to Paul in his letter to the Romans (chapters 9–11), but as the new Israel that has replaced the old according to the gospel of John and the letter to the Hebrews where this is a strong and central theme. For all of that, the church still knows that her Messiah was sent to his own people Israel. Jesus believed in the God of Abraham, Isaac, and Jacob. His followers are children of that same God. For Jews, Christians, and Muslims, Abraham is our common father in faith. To deny the Jewish rootedness of the church would be to deny Jesus himself.

Q. 52. Why was Jesus so strict with his own disciples, telling them to hate their families and not even to go back home to say goodbye or to bury the dead?

Jesus' sayings about discipleship would have been shocking even to his contemporaries: not to have a place to lay one's head, i.e. a home; not to perform the most sacred of duties, to bury one's own father; not even to go home and say farewell to one's family (Lk 9:57–62 par.)! Even worse is the saying a little further on in Luke: "Whoever comes to me and does not hate father and mother, wife and children, brothers and sisters, yes, and even life itself, cannot be my disciple" (Lk 14:26 par.).

St. Ignatius, in the *Spiritual Exercises,* speaks of "indifference." He does not mean what the word often connotes in English, i.e. an uncaring attitude or a passive acquiescence with regard to what happens to oneself or to one's family. Ignatius was a passionate man, as was Jesus. He is talking about a profound and radical involvement in God's love, so intense, so personal, so deep that everything else on the face of the earth takes on meaning and importance only in the light of this relationship. Hence, "indifference" might be better translated as "radical single-mindedness," like the dog waiting for the morsel to fall from the table with every fibre of her being tense with attention and expectation (Mk 7:28 par.). This concentration of one's whole being is recognized as faith (Mt 15:28). Jesus is not denying the beauty, goodness, and desirability of family, home, and honor for father and mother. God's love does not negate or destroy the goodness of human life. Rather, it is God's love in our hearts that enables us and empowers us to love others in a way that is truly fulfilling.

For Jesus and his disciples, this "radical single-mindedness" takes the concrete shape of proclaiming and working for the kingdom of God. Other concerns, even life itself, will be seen in their proper light and brought to true fulfillment if the disciples seek first the kingdom of God and the righteousness of God (Mt 6:25–33 par.). It should be noted, finally, that this radical single-mindedness is for all those who claim to follow Jesus, whether they travel with him on the way or remain in their homes (see Q. 27). It is not just for priests and religious, as later generations have sometimes thought. The so-called "evangelical counsels" of poverty, chastity, and obedience are for all Christians, though the lifestyle that gives shape to them will depend on the particular vocation of each person.

Q. 53. If Jesus was sent to proclaim the kingdom of God and yet failed, did he know all along that he would have to die for us?

We have been maintaining that Jesus in his historical and human life was a man like us in all things, tested and tempted as we are. This would mean that he experienced doubts and uncertainties, that he had to explore the best way to communicate the message the Father had given him, that he had to trust in the Father's will when things weren't turning out as hoped, that he had to face the very real possibility of failure and death. One can well imagine that the growing opposition and hostility that he was experiencing led him to consider not only the possibility but the probability of a violent death. In true prophetic fashion, the crisis of human rejection evoked the hope of divine vindication, i.e. that no matter what happened God would vindicate his mission and bring the kingdom to fulfillment. This may have been the import for Jesus of the image: "the Day of the Son of Man" (Lk 17:24). In the book of Daniel, "one like a son of man" (7:14), i.e. a human figure in contrast to the four beasts representing the imperial powers that have persecuted the people of God, comes before the throne of God and receives divine vindication. Just so, Jesus had to trust that his Father would vindicate him.

Hence, Jesus was a man of faith who believed that "all things are possible" for one who believes (Mk 9:23), for God (Mk 10:27), and for his *Abba* (Mk 14:36). For one who has faith like a grain of mustard seed, nothing is impossible. Such a one can move the mountain of human hard-heartedness (Mt 17:20) and uproot the notably deep-rooted tree of human intransigence (Lk 17:6). Faith has improbable power, like the mustard seed which is the smallest of all seeds and still produces the greatest of all shrubs (Mk 4:31–32 par.). Jesus did not know exactly when, where, and how he would die, but he did know that the power of God (Mk 12:24) and the power of faith (Mk 5:36) will defeat fear and death and bring forth new life. The poignancy of Jesus' prayer in the garden was his felt need to find the strength to remain faithful to this God of love and life in the face of fear and death. The final petition of the Lord's Prayer (as at Lk 11:4 par.) may well mean: Give us the strength not to fail at the time of the trial! Jesus and his disciples both needed such strength.

Q. 54. But didn't Jesus predict his death before it happened?

In the gospel of Mark, after Peter's confession of faith (8:27–30), Jesus tells the disciples three times that the Son of Man must undergo great suffering, be rejected and killed, and rise again after three days (Mk 8:31 par.; 9:31 par.; 10:33–34 par.). Matthew and Luke follow Mark in this. Even John has such a threefold prediction (Jn 3:14–15; 8:28; 12:32), but in his own image of the Son of Man being "lifted up," i.e. exalted on the cross. For Mark, as for John, the cross is the moment or "hour" in which Jesus' true identity is fully and finally revealed. The predictions are an anticipation of that hour and remain obscure and puzzling until the events actually take place. In Mark, for example, after Peter says: "You are the Messiah," Jesus immediately orders them not to tell anyone about him, i.e. about his true identity, for even the disciples cannot yet understand that "Messiah" for him means the crucified Messiah. Jesus first must teach them about the necessity of the cross, which Peter immediately denies, and which then becomes the occasion for instruction about taking up the cross and following him. This is what being a true disciple means. This pattern of prediction, denial, and instruction on discipleship is repeated, with variations, three times. Clearly, this is the central teaching section of Mark's whole gospel. The religious and theological point he wants to make is clear: we Christians will never understand who Jesus is and inseparably who we are as disciples unless we are willing to take up the cross and experience for ourselves how he died (Mk 15:39). Only then can we truly say that he is the "Christ" and the "Son of God." These titles take on their true significance only in the light of the cross. Thus, it is not the titles that interpret Jesus' significance for us. Rather, it is the cross that gives meaning to the titles. Mark's gospel, like the parables of Jesus (see Q. 35), does not give us information but calls us to participation in Jesus' way to the cross.

Do the predictions in some form go back to Jesus himself? The witness of all four gospels is a strong indicator that they do. I find convincing the view of Joachim Jeremias that underlying the second prediction at Mark 9:31a is an original riddle in Aramaic: "The Son of Man is being handed over into the hands of the sons of men." This is a play on words using "Son of Man" not as a formal Christological title but as a generic reference meaning something like "a man like myself," i.e. one having the particular mission and experience that I have. In this sense, it refers not only to Jesus but to all those who participate in his mission as disciples. On the lips of Jesus, the saying would be a prophetic riddle meant to convey the present experience of crisis and conflict that would include the very real probability of violent death. In any case, it would not be the clear predictions after the fact that we now have in the gospels. Jesus still had to have faith that God will provide a resolution to the crisis. His image for this resolution is "the Day of the Son of Man" (Lk 17:24).

Q. 55. Why was there so much opposition to Jesus? Why would the Jews want to kill him? And what difference would it make to the Romans?

First of all, we must be careful about the categories we use. In the synoptic gospels, the phrase "the Jews" is used principally in reference to the inscription on the cross: "the king of the Jews." Jesus' principal opponents are the leaders of the people: the chief priests, the scribes and Pharisees, the Herodians (although eventually the disciples also desert him and the crowds turn against him at the instigation of the leaders). In John's gospel, the phrase "the Jews" is frequently used as a convenient summary for all of Jesus' opponents. Unfortunately, in later Christian history, this phrase was picked up and used as a justification for the terrible and tragic history of antisemitism. It should be noted that in John Jesus is called "a Jew" (4:9), "salvation is from the Jews" (4:22), and there are Jews who believed in him (8:31; 11:45; 12:11). Of course, not only Jesus but all of his first disciples, e.g. Peter and the twelve, were Jewish.

Thus, Jesus was a Jew brought to his death by certain other Jews who saw him as a threat to their power and privilege. Historically, Jesus seems to have had relatively congenial relations with the scribes and Pharisees, with whom he could engage in serious conversation about the law. The portrayal of the scribes and Pharisees in the gospels as principal opponents may have had more to do with the fact that, after the destruction of the temple in 70, the religion of Israel survived as rabbinic Judaism, the apparent heirs to the scribes and Pharisees as preservers and interpreters of the law (see Q. 29). The gospels were written during the last third of the first century and frequently reflect the controversies the authors and their communities were facing then.

Jesus most likely faced the greatest opposition from the temple aristocracy (the chief priests and the Sadducees) and from the puppet kings (the Herodians) because they were in collusion with the Roman occupying power and were dependent on the Romans for their positions of power and wealth. Jesus challenged the power structures of his day by calling for a renewed and revitalized Israel that would overturn the hegemony of the powerful and create a new kind of community, thus heralding the arrival of God's kingdom in opposition to that of Caesar or his collaborators. It is not hard to see that the Romans would perceive a threat to the priests and the Herodians as a threat to their own system and so would consider Jesus a rebel (see Q. 39).

Q. 56. There was a lot of controversy surrounding the movie "The Last Temptation of Christ." What do you think of it? Did Jesus have a last temptation?

Martin Scorsese made the film because he was deeply impressed by a novel of the same title written by Nikos Kazantzakis, a Greek author, in 1955. Scorsese remains very faithful to the book which, as in all of Kazantzakis' writings, revolves around the very Greek preoccupation with the struggle between flesh and spirit. In this case, the central theme is the temptation of Jesus' humanity against his divinity, i.e. Jesus is portrayed on the cross as tempted to forsake his messiahship, come down from the cross, and live a normal human life as a married man with children. This temptation is presented in the form of a fantasy going on in Jesus' mind while he is enduring his torments on the cross. In the end, he overcomes the temptation and triumphs as Messiah.

A number of observations can be made. First, many people considered the movie blasphemous because they took it to be an attempt to portray the Jesus whom we know from the gospels. This does not seem to be the intention of either the book or the film. Some may be offended that the figure of Jesus was used, but it does portray a universal human experience as a real possibility in Jesus' life. We have already said that his temptations were real experiences for him (see Q. 38). What a film like this does is allow us to expand our imaginations, to see Jesus in a more human perspective. While the film is not a literal portrayal of even one of the gospels, it does offer an imaginative and moving portrayal of the kinds of struggles that Jesus too had to face.

Second, there are many films about Jesus that are far worse because they portray him as a blond, blue-eyed, saccharine wimp! By way of contrast, I would highly recommend Pier Paolo Pasolini's film "The Gospel According to St. Matthew." It is a fine example of artistic imagination oriented around and controlled by a primary source.

Finally, it makes Jesus appear a bit schizophrenic to portray his temptations as a struggle of his humanity against his divinity. It tends to play humanity off against divinity in a competitive fashion. While I would not endorse any approach that makes the divine and the human appear to be in competition with each other, the biblical tradition does seem to talk on the reverse side of a temptation of the divinity against humanity, e.g. in the story of Noah. God is sorry to have made human beings because of their wickedness and decides to blot them out (Gen 6:5–8; cf. 6:11–13.17; 7:23). But God's faithful love eventually wins out (Gen 9:8–17; cp. Ps 79:5 with Ps 86:15; 103:8; 145:8).

Q. 57. What about the abandonment on the cross? Would Jesus have been tempted against God then?

The only word of Jesus on the cross in Mark and Matthew is: "My God, my God, why have you forsaken me?" (Mk 15:34 = Mt 27:46). Jesus is citing the opening verse of Psalm 22, a prayer for deliverance by someone facing a sickness unto death. It is difficult to know if Jesus actually said the words, although many have wondered why Mark would invent them. Certainly the tendency of the tradition to use other sayings on the cross is evident in Luke and John who omit this saying. However historical the cry of abandonment may be, we can certainly ponder its theological meaning for Mark and for us.

According to Mark, Jesus died rejected and abandoned not only by the leaders of the people, by his family and friends at Nazareth, by his disciples and the crowds who had eagerly followed after him—so that he had to face death totally and utterly alone—but even by the God in whom he trusted and whose kingdom he came to proclaim. Mark draws the curtain on Jesus' human life with an unrelieved focus on abandonment. At this point, while we need not speculate about the actual state of Jesus' mind at the moment of his death, we can ask: What theological sense can we make of his abandonment and does it have anything to do with a "last temptation"?

Paul, reflecting on the significance of Jesus' whole life and not necessarily on any particular moment, says that God sent his own Son "in the likeness of sinful flesh, to deal with sin . . ." (Rom 8:3; cp. Phil 2:6–8), and, even more strikingly, "for our sake he made him to be sin who knew no sin . . ." (2 Cor 5:21). I take this to mean that Jesus' whole life and especially the moment of his death was an ever-growing and deepening identification with us in our sinful human condition "so that in him we might become the righteousness of God" (2 Cor 5:21). Jesus experienced the full impact of human sin. "The LORD has laid on him the iniquity of us all" (Is 53:6). He descended into the depths of human sinfulness where even the Father, whose involvement in creation is intrinsically and absolutely good, could not follow. In this sense, one could say that the Father, not by some arbitrary choice but by a necessity that human sin had created, had to abandon him, had to let him become sin for the sake of human freedom and human transformation (which is the "righteousness of God" of which Paul speaks at 2 Cor 5:21).

It is in this experience that one could meaningfully speak of a "last temptation" or, perhaps better, of the temptation that coursed through his whole life but received its focal intensity in his death. It was not a temptation against the God who sent him, the God he knew as a loving and caring *Abba*. The cry on the cross remains a cry of trust. Rather, I think, it was a temptation against those to whom he was sent. Jesus, in effect, had to remain faithful to *us*. Overwhelmed by our capacity for evil, crushed by the intensity of our enmity toward him, he freely chose despite our sinfulness to love us and to remain faithful to us. We know this, not because we can enter into his state of mind at any particular moment, but because God raised him from the dead. Here, in Jesus' free and faithful love for us *while we were his enemies,* it makes sense to call him our Savior (cp.

Rom 5:6–11). On the cross, we see fulfilled his own command: "Love your enemies!"

Q. 58. Could you say something more about what you mean by sin?

God's intention in creating is the good of creation as a whole. A wonderful phrase of St. Irenaeus, "The glory of God is the human person made fully alive" (to paraphrase a bit), captures the divine intention well. God does not compete with us, but seeks always to bring us to the fullness of who we are as human beings. We sin when, in one way or another, we seek to destroy or subvert this creative intention of God. We do not directly offend God so much as we destroy God's good creation. The symbol of the tree of the knowledge of good and evil, as the story of Genesis 2–3 unfolds, has to do with our relations as human beings to God, to nature, and to one another. The desire to be like God is the desire to replace God with oneself, so that we can determine good and evil apart from God. This to make ourselves something we can never be.

Sin is not just a question of my personal relationship with God. Sin constitutes the human condition such that we are born into a world in which our very identity as persons takes shape within a continuing struggle between the forces of evil (sin) and the power of good (grace). The whole history of Israel reflects this struggle. For Christians, that history culminates in the decisive moment of the cross. It is not the disobedience of Adam and Eve so much as the rejection and murder of God's beloved Son (Mk 12:1–8) that is the full symbolic evocation of human sin, of the terrible abyss of our human capacity for evil. The full meaning and impact of the "original sin" is revealed in the cross of Jesus. Here is where the abandonment of God can make sense. It is not that God has a positive will to abandon us. Rather, by our sin we abandon God, and God, who has created us to be free, respects the dignity and integrity of our human freedom even when it may create an unbridgeable chasm between God and the sinner (Lk 16:26). Indeed, if the Jewish and Christian scriptures tell us anything, it is that God does not impose the divine will on recalcitrant creatures but continually invites a free and loving response. Thus, the drama of salvation, or true human liberation, is played out in human freedom—both Jesus' human freedom and our own.

Q. 59. But why would God do that to his innocent Son? Why did the Father want Jesus to die so young and in such a horrifying and humiliating manner?

The question of divine providence becomes acute when we look at the cross of Jesus. I have found useful an image borrowed from my former mentor, John H. Wright, S.J., namely the "God who dialogues." It involves three steps. First, there is the divine initiative. God is the alpha and the omega. Everything comes from God and returns to God. This is what we mean when we call God Creator. Second, there is the human response to the divine initiative, which can be either positive (a gracious response) or negative (a sinful response). Third, there is the divine response to the human response. This means that God has created a world in which God has freely chosen to respect the dignity and integrity of our human freedom even when it leads to destructive action. In a word, God has created a world in which God as Creator truly depends on our free human response to the divine initiative in order to give shape to the world in which we live. It makes a profound difference to God what we do! We can either build the earth and so realize the divine intention through gradual transformation or we can destroy the earth and so realize the divine intention through cataclysmic destruction. The point is: the options are real but in either case ultimately the divine intention will be realized. However, the divine intention is being realized here and now through us. The future shape of God's kingdom depends on whether we choose to be co-creators with God of that future or not.

The cross is where we see this providential pattern most fully realized. In my view, the Father did not send his Son into the world to die on the cross. Only a monstrous God would do such a thing. The Father sent his Son to proclaim the depth of the Father's love and the realization of that love in a kingdom of transforming grace. The human response to this divine initiative was twofold. On the part of Jesus, it was to remain faithful (obedient) to the mission given him even unto death. On the part of his enemies, it was to reject the divine initiative and crucify God's beloved Son. Thus, it was not God who created the cross but human beings. In this way, the cross is first a symbol of human sinfulness and only as such can it be seen as a continuing offer of divine love. The divine response to Jesus' fidelity and to the tragedy of human rejection was to raise Jesus from the dead. The Father's embrace of his beloved Son in the power of the Spirit at the moment of his rejection and abandonment means that God remains faithful in love despite our human sinfulness. But it also means that we live from that day to this under the sign of the cross—a sign of human tragedy.

Q. 60. Don't the scriptures say that God wanted Jesus to die on the cross?

There are many passages in scripture that seem to indicate this: the language of God "sending" or "giving" his only Son; the emphasis on divine necessity, i.e. that the Son of Man *must* suffer and die, in the passion predictions (see Q. 54); the prayer of Jesus in the garden that the Father's will be done. Certainly, the idea that God sent Jesus in order to die on the cross and so save us from our sins has been a common interpretation. In the interests of ongoing interpretation, however, two things can be said.

First, the NT authors are writing from a perspective after the fact. They already know that Jesus has died on the cross and they seek to interpret that fact as the fulfillment of the OT scriptures and thus as part of God's total plan. " 'Was it not necessary that the Messiah should suffer these things and then enter into his glory?' Then beginning with Moses and all the prophets, he interpreted to them the things about himself in all the scriptures" (Lk 24:26–27; cp. vv. 44–49). Luke never indicates exactly which scriptures are being referred to in this chapter, but the point is that Jesus' death and resurrection fulfill the meaning of the scriptures as a whole. The early church did employ specific OT texts to defend the claim that Jesus was not only Messiah but was such precisely as crucified. This was indeed the critical apologetic question. How could the one who had been cursed by God by hanging on a tree now be the blessing of God (Gal 3:13–14)? Two early texts employed were Psalm 118:22, on human rejection and divine vindication, and Isaiah 53, the song of the suffering servant. The notion of God's plan was eventually elaborated in comprehensive and cosmic terms. God "has made known to us the mystery of his will, according to his good pleasure that he set forth in Christ, as a plan for the fullness of time, to gather up all things in him, things in heaven and things on earth" (Eph 1:9–10).

The second point is a corollary to the first. The biblical authors of both the OT and the NT do not make a clear distinction between what God wills and what God permits. Everything is finally attributed to God as the only cause, the Creator of all that is. The image of the "God who dialogues" is a much later interpretation that recognizes that God's causality is mediated through human causality, i.e. that God brings about the divine will through us. This involves a risk even for God because it puts much greater stress on human freedom as conditioning the success or failure of the divine intention. Hence, as mentioned earlier, Jesus failed in his historical mission, and that failure was reversed by the divine response of resurrection.

Q. 61. Isn't it God who saves us? What does human freedom have to do with it?

Salvation is certainly the central issue in our understanding of Jesus. The fathers of the church maintained, as an argument for Jesus' divinity, that only God can save us and, as an argument for his full humanity, that only what is united with the divine can be saved. This is good as far as it goes, but it assumes that salvation takes place at the "moment" of the incarnation, i.e. when the divine and the human are united in Jesus, when "the Word became flesh" (Jn 1:14). But even John recognizes that the prologue is not enough; he must tell the full story of Jesus and especially his way to the cross.

The image of the "God who dialogues" recognizes that salvation is from God. Everything begins in the divine initiative and ends in the divine response. Only God can save us. The question is, rather: *How* does God save us? Taking a clue from Jesus' proclamation of the kingdom in parables, it seems that God is at work—alive, active, present—in the midst of human life, and particularly in the human life of Jesus. God our Savior, says 1 Timothy 2:4–6, "desires everyone to be saved and to come to the knowledge of the truth; for there is one God; there is also one mediator between God and humankind, Christ Jesus, himself a human, who gave himself a ransom for all." I take this to mean that Jesus mediates between God and us precisely in his *humanness.* God brings about the divine intention for universal salvation in and through the human freedom of Jesus. It is not a question of playing divinity off against humanity in a competitive manner but of seeing that God has accepted and identified as God's own this human life in all its concreteness and particularity, with all the sufferings and temptations and struggles to remain faithful to the mission given him that we see reflected in the gospels. Jesus was called by the God whom he characterized as a loving and caring *Abba* to remain faithful to us (as God is ever faithful love) in and despite the devastation of human sin. To say that Jesus is our Savior is to say that he transformed, *from within* our human condition, the disobedience of Adam into the obedience of God's only Son. God's covenant with creation is constituted once and for all in the singular freedom of Jesus, the faithful one. It is in and through his own freedom and for the sake of our freedom that "Christ has set us free" (Gal 5:1).

Q. 62. Was it essential for Jesus to suffer on the cross for our sins? Why couldn't each of us just take responsibility for our own actions to gain salvation? Isn't it enough if we repent and follow the teachings of Jesus?

If we humans are truly free to make choices, the response to Jesus could have been different. There was no absolute necessity, divine or human, that Jesus should die on the cross. The only necessity for the cross derives from the actual, specific situation in which Jesus found himself. And, although it is hypothetical given the fact of the cross, we can imagine what the world today might be like had the response to Jesus been other than rejection and crucifixion.

The question, however, implies something else that stems from our individualistic culture, namely that we can save ourselves by our own efforts. It is true that each of us must repent and follow not only the teachings of Jesus but, more to the point, his whole way of life. Salvation is not automatic. It demands our personal participation in the process of transformation, but as a *response* to the divine initiative. Faith has always been understood as the free gift of God (a grace) that enables us to respond even as it is understood as our response. Moreover, we must remember that our struggle for liberation is more than just an individual one; it is against the pervasive and systemic power of evil imaged as "Satan" (see Q. 40). In our western culture, we tend to think of ourselves first as individuals and then as relating to various groupings, e.g. family, church, civil society, etc. But, for Jesus and the semitic culture from which he came, one's first sense of personal identity is with the community, and only then does one consider one's individual identity. This is important for our understanding of salvation. In a very real sense, all of us are in this together so that no one of us is saved until all of us are saved. The salvation that God seeks in Jesus is the transformation of society and indeed of the whole creation (Rom 8:18–25), a "new creation" catalyzed by the experience of love and reconciliation in the Christian community (2 Cor 5:14–20; Gal 6:14–15).

Jesus is integral and necessary to God's salvific intention for two reasons. First, his freely given obedience even unto death accepted in the transformative power of the resurrection means that God's intention for human beings from the beginning of creation has been realized in him. He is the "Son of Man," the new human being. Second, as such he is the "first fruits" of all who will be made alive in him (1 Cor 15:20–28), i.e. he communicates to us the gracious power of his Spirit which empowers us and enables us to live as he lived, to participate in his way and so bring to realization the full transformation and liberation intended by God from the beginning of creation. Once again, God works from within creation to realize the divine will and does not impose that will from outside. What we do makes a difference for the salvation of the world!

Q. 63. If salvation is still future, why did Jesus say "it is finished"?

Let me note first that we have three quite different presentations of Jesus' words on the cross in the gospels. Mark and Matthew have only the one saying about abandonment (see Q. 57). The moment of Jesus' death is a moment of darkness and tragedy. Luke, on the other hand, continues the image of Jesus at prayer, asking forgiveness for those who are killing him (23:34), offering salvation to the criminal who defended him (23:43), and finally committing himself totally into the hands of the Father (23:46). The moment of Jesus' death is a moment of forgiveness and reconciliation. For John, Jesus continues to be the master of his own destiny, lifted up and enthroned on the cross (18:33–37; 19:11.19–22), drawing all people to himself (12:42). Jesus fulfills the hopes of Israel by entrusting her, in the person of his mother, to the church in the person of the beloved disciple (19:26–27; see Q. 18). Knowing that all had now been fulfilled, he ensures the fulfillment of scripture by saying: "I am thirsty" (19:28). Finally, he pronounces that it is so, saying: "It is finished" (19:30). One must read the words on the cross in John in the light of Jesus' farewell discourses and prayer (chapters 13–17). In the prayer Jesus says that he has finished the work the Father gave him to do (17:4). Now he goes to sanctify himself so that his followers may be sanctified in truth (17:19). The moment of his death is the moment when he fulfills all that he had come to do and hands over the Spirit (19:30) so that his followers may live on in the truth (14:15–17.26; 15:26; 16:13–15).

From the perspective I have been suggesting, Jesus is indeed the one in whom the divine creative intention for universal salvation has been realized. He is the unique Savior. Only by living in the Spirit that he has "poured out" (Acts 2:33) can we hope to bring to full realization the transformation and liberation already fully in him but not yet fully in us, so that at the end of the process he can hand over the kingdom to the Father and "God may be all in all" (1

Cor 15:28). In this way, we bring to completion what is lacking in the sufferings of Christ (Col 1:24).

Q. 64. Did Jesus' death really prove or accomplish anything? Looking at the world today, it doesn't seem to have done any good. Has anything changed?

Whatever else we say about it, history does involve real change. But it involves zigs and zags, regressions, insights lost, lapses, reversals, rediscoveries, new departures. At any given moment, it is impossible to say whether things are getting better or worse. Philosophers have developed grand theories about history. The optimists would have us believe that we are always progressing, despite some temporary setbacks and rough edges, toward an ever new utopia. The pessimists, on the other hand, see the world going to hell in a handbasket. We are cabined, cribbed, and confined—and it's getting worse all the time. These views have as much to do with genes and natural inclinations as with the possible validity of any theory.

For a Christian, the question brings us back to the way we conceive divine providence. As suggested already (see Q. 59), God does not pre-determine in some fixed fashion the shape of things to come but rather invites us to create with God a better future for all. God works within the possibilities of our human freedom and accepts its limitations (including the human freedom of Jesus). The important point is that the options between building the earth or destroying it are real. This means that in contrast to either the optimistic or the pessimistic persuasion we should adopt a *realistic* point of view. If the options are real, it makes a difference what we do for the shape of things to come. We are not innocent bystanders.

On the other hand, Christians ground their hope for a better future in the Spirit of the risen Jesus. His Spirit enables and empowers us but we must respond and take responsibility for the life entrusted to us. It is faith that assures us of what we hope for, that convinces us of what we have not yet seen (Heb 11:1), but such faith and hope, if it is to be true and not just wishful thinking, must be grounded in actual experience. If we hope that Jesus' Spirit will triumph, it is because we experience the transformative power of that Spirit in our own lives and loves.

Q. 65. But why does there need to be so much suffering and evil in the world? Isn't it all rather meaningless for people who suffer from misfortunes or diseases or poverty?

Paul says: "If for this life only we have hoped in Christ, we are of all people most to be pitied" (1 Cor 15:19). Unfortunately, this has often been interpreted as advocating a passive acquiescence in evil, waiting for the pie in the sky when we die. Paul, like Jesus before him, knew that we must confront those evils that lie within human capabilities, both in ourselves and in others. We hope for the final transformation of all things in Christ (Phil 3:10.21) but we know that such transformation has begun in our baptism which enables us to "walk in newness of life" (Rom 6:4).

Such hope does not do away with the mystery of evil; it rather emphasizes it. Evil is not a problem that has a rational solution because evil is by nature irrational. All attempts to rationalize evil and fit it into some higher system of thought have failed. You cannot rationalize the irrational. The question often asked: Why did God let this happen to me? admits of no answer. As difficult as it is, the only question that is feasible in the midst of a tragic event is: What can or should I do now that this has happened? How can this too work together with all things for good (Rom 8:28)?

In scripture God gives us two answers to the question of evil, neither of them perhaps the ones we want. In the book of Job, the only answer that finally comes forth is that evil itself is enshrouded in the mystery of that same God who answers out of the whirlwind (Job 38:1ff; 40:6ff). There are some evils, e.g. natural catastrophes, that are simply out of our control and beyond our understanding. But what about those evils that come from the human heart and can be changed? God's second answer is to send his beloved Son who walks in solidarity with the most miserable and oppressed and who suffers what they suffer even to the death of an outcast and criminal on the cross. There is no theoretical answer to the question of suffering. God's only answer is to walk with us on the way, a new way of truth and life that seeks to overcome the power of sin and death from within the human heart.

Q. 66. If Jesus is God and suffered on the cross, does that mean that God suffers?

This, of course, is the classic problem that confronted the church fathers. If we maintain the fullness of humanity and the fullness of divinity in the unity of one person, then we must say that the Son of God suffered and died on the cross (as we do say in the Creed). The approach commonly taken, e.g. by St. Athanasius, the great defender of Nicene orthodoxy, is to say that Jesus suffered in his humanity (or "flesh") but not in his divinity. This is based on the Greek notion of perfection. Any sort of change or becoming, but especially suffering, implies imperfection. This was Arius' problem (see Q. 15): How can we say "the Word became flesh" and still maintain that the Word is fully divine? The scriptures, on the other hand, are not concerned with an abstract ideal of perfection but with the living God who "knew" in a personal and intimate way (Ex 2:23–25) the sufferings of the people and who sought to free them from oppression. This is a God of compassionate love who walks with the people, covenants with them, endures their rejection, and brings them to the promised land. The God of Israel is not distant and apathetic, uncaring and unaffected by the fortunes of the beloved community. This God is deeply involved and deeply affected by the history of Israel and indeed by the history of all peoples.

For Christians, God's self-involvement in creation and covenant culminates with the personal history of Jesus, God's only and beloved Son, given to us out of the depths of divine love (Jn 3:16; Rom 8:31–39). Many theologians today, returning to a more biblically based understanding, affirm that indeed God suffers in Jesus. But God suffers as God, not as creatures. There is no attempt here, as was the Greek fear, to reduce God to the level of creatures. On the other hand, God has been so foolish as to create a world in which the divine Self is deeply and personally involved. It does make a difference to God what we do and what we suffer. Like the artist who is inextricably identified with and intertwined with his or her artistic creation, God as Creator has fashioned a world that is God's own, God's "place," God's very body, i.e. the self-expression of divine creativity. If the Son suffers death out of obedient love, then, however difficult it may be to understand, the Father suffers that same death out of the fullness of divine love.

Q. 67. Didn't God overcome the death of Jesus in the resurrection? The cross is a past event. Shouldn't we put more stress on the resurrection?

If Jesus had only died on the cross, despised as a failure and crucified as a criminal, I doubt that we would be talking about him today. The resurrection gives meaning to the cross as the revelation of God's willing acceptance of this human life and death as God's own. But, on the other hand, the cross gives meaning to the resurrection. We are not talking about the general expectation of resurrection at the end-time, which some of Jesus' contemporaries believed to be coming, but about the resurrection of *this man* Jesus of Nazareth, condemned as a blasphemer by many of his own people, crucified as a rebel by the Roman occupying power, and having died cursed and abandoned by God (Gal 3:13; Mk 15:34 par.). The cross and resurrection, though distinguishable moments, form one inseparable event. The image of the father running down the path, embracing his son and covering him with kisses in the parable of the man who had two sons (Lk 15:11–32) is for me a powerful and moving image of the resurrection. In Jesus' case, the Son though innocent has "become sin," suffering the full effects of our human capacity for evil. The Father, at the moment of the Son's death, embraces him with the creative, transforming power of the Spirit. God remains faithful in love even in the face of human enmity and rejection. The divine response to human hardness of heart is to continue being what God is by nature: "faithful love" (Ps 89:1–2; a common theme throughout the Jewish scriptures).

The two dimensions of human fidelity and divine fidelity must remain inseparable in the event of cross-resurrection. This human life, from the moment of conception to the moment of death, with all the struggles and temptations as well as joys and victories, is God's own human life. It is not that Jesus' human life shows us one possible way to achieve true human liberation; it is now declared to be the *only* way. But that human life has its origins in God's faithful love: conceived in the power of the Spirit, anointed by the Spirit, "declared to be Son of God with power according to the Spirit of holiness by resurrection from the dead" (Rom 1:4). We know that Jesus remained faithful to us, obedient to the divine mission given him, because God raised him from the dead. It is the whole of his life, but especially his fidelity on the cross, that has transformed the human condition and enabled us to become God's children in him (Rom 8:12–17). His human fidelity, however, has its origin and its end in the divine fidelity. It is God's embrace of this human life and death as God's own that conquers the power of death and gives newness of life.

Q. 68. Are you saying that Jesus was not God until the resurrection?

No, but what I am saying is that whatever we mean when we call Jesus God must engage fully his human life. Jesus, by reason of his unity with the divine, is not somehow less human than we are. On the contrary, it is precisely his union with the divine that makes him most fully human, the "human One" or "Son of Man," who fully but in a way unique to him realizes God's creative intention for all humanity. What he *is* by nature, we *have* by adoption (or participation) in him (Rom 8:15). What the resurrection reveals primarily is the fullness of what it is to be human. Jesus is not somehow less human because divine; rather it is we who are less human because alienated and separated from the divine. Sin does not make us human; it dehumanizes us because it cuts us off from the only source of true humanness, the God of Jesus alive, active, present in our hearts and in all our relationships.

The resurrection, then, brings to completion or fulfillment God's creative intention for humankind. Paul, using the contrasting imagery of apocalyptic (the difference between this world and the world to come), says that what is sown is "a physical body." He refers to Genesis 2:7 where the first human being (Adam) was created out of the dust from the ground and the divine breath (Spirit) so that what was formed became "a living being." This is the normal, human "Adamic" existence that all of us, and most especially Jesus, experience. But, as Paul elaborates in Romans, chapters 5–7, this human life is subjected to the power of sin (chapter 5), death (chapter 6), and law (chapter 7). By contrast, what is raised, says Paul, is "a spiritual body" (as it is often translated at 1 Cor 15:44). I take this to mean that what is raised is in bodily continuity (*sōma* = body, used in both expressions) with what was sown, but now that same "embodied person" has been transformed by the creative power of God's Spirit. It is a new creation, a new human being.

Traditionally, we have spoken of three gifts which Adam and Eve had and lost, namely sanctifying grace (union with the divine), integrity (full and harmonious exercise of the human faculties without any tendency toward concupiscence or weakness of the flesh), and immortality (in the sense of not being subject to the power of death). Correspondingly, each of these gifts has its opposite: sin–law–death (as elaborated by Paul in Romans, chapters 5–7). However we understand the story of Adam and Eve, it is certainly true for Paul that God has conquered the power of sin, law, and death in the resurrection of Jesus (1 Cor 15:56–57; Rom 8). In my view, Jesus as risen has realized in himself and hence made available to all humans by way of participation the full and final transformation of the human condition (1 Cor 15:51–52): union with the divine, a fully integrated human existence, and victory over the final enemy death.

Q. 69. Does Jesus have the same body now that he had before he died?

Paul addressed this question. He said that someone will ask: "How are the dead raised? With what kind of body do they come?"

(1 Cor 15:35). He says, in effect, that this is a foolish question but then goes on for several verses (vv. 35–57) explaining what he means. He draws on analogies from nature to show that there are diverse kinds of bodies. The important point is that God gives each one its own body as God has freely chosen. The whole of creation and especially resurrection depends on the divine creativity. His basic point is to show the contrast between what is sown and what is raised, but this contrast also implies continuity as a human transformation (vv. 51–53; Phil 3:21).

One thing is certain: a risen body is not a resuscitated corpse, i.e. a return to this life so that one must still face death as in the case of Lazarus (Jn 11:38–44; 12:10). Paul does not try to give a physical description of a risen body. Rather, he elaborates its theological significance as God's victory over sin, law, and death. But the metaphor of resurrection ("waking from sleep") is important. Immortality in the sense of a separation of the spiritual soul which can live forever from the limitations of the physical body is a Greek idea. The Hebrew image of resurrection is more wholistic. It refers to the whole person as inseparably an *embodied* spirit. When Paul uses *sōma* (body), he is referring to the whole person. The same body-person who lived through the normal human life-span from birth to death continues to live beyond death, but now in risen glory as transformed by the creative power of God's Spirit. Continuity includes both identity (the same person) and difference (human transformation). We cannot describe in physical terms what a risen body is like. We can only speak of it by way of analogy with our normal human experiences, affirming at the same time that it utterly transcends our experience. A good analogy is our own personal experience of growth and development. We know that we are the same person we were at the moment of birth and yet we also know that we have changed radically.

A final note: the significance of bodily resurrection should not be limited to our individual selves. Jesus' resurrection is the beginning of the transformation of the whole of creation. Thus, the full meaning of resurrection will only be known when all creatures great and small are transformed into Christ. The early church recognized in a wonderful hymn (Col 1:15–20) that if Jesus was "the firstborn from the dead," then he was also "the firstborn of all creation."

Q. 70. I've heard some people call the risen Jesus the "cosmic Christ." What does that mean?

Very quickly, in the light of the resurrection, the early church perceived that the Lordship of the risen Christ extended to the whole of creation. The resurrection is sometimes called an "eschatological event," i.e. it is the final and decisive act of God's creativity for the whole of creation. If Jesus as risen is identified with the final and decisive act of God's creativity, then by implication he is identified with the whole of God's creativity from beginning to end. In other words, he is identified with the whole cosmos.

This is the dynamic of the early hymn we find incorporated into the letter to the Colossians (1:15–20). The hymn has two main parts which mutually interpret each other. The first part (vv. 15–18b), which begins: "He is the image of the invisible God, the firstborn of all creation . . ." explores the cosmic implications of the resurrection. All things have been created in him, through him, and for him so that he sustains the entire universe. The second part (vv. 18c–20), which begins: "He is the beginning, the firstborn from the dead . . ." affirms that it is his resurrection which constitutes his pre-eminence over all things. Thus, it is the resurrection, the fullness of God's reconciling love in him, that now gives him dominion and power over all the earth, both the living and the dead. According to 1 Peter 3:18–22 (which contains fragments of another early hymn), the risen Jesus "made alive in the Spirit" preached in the realm of the dead to those "who in former times did not obey." The risen Lord has power that stretches back to ancestors and moves forward toward the final victory over "the cosmic powers" (Eph 6:12; cp. 1 Cor 15:20–28).

The biblical language is at times stark and apocalyptic: a struggle against enemies that are hostile and evil and that have great powers of their own. At other times, it is loving and reconciliatory: a peaceful transformation of all things in Christ. Rather than play one image off against another as if they were contradictory, it seems to me more helpful to take the realistic view (see Q. 64). Both are real possibilities. The final shape of the world to come will depend on how we respond to the mystery of the divine intention "set forth in Christ" (Eph 1:9).

Q. 71. If Jesus has such power now, why didn't he just stay on earth and continue to help us out?

The beginning of Acts poses a similar question when the apostles ask: "Lord, is this the time when you will restore the kingdom to Israel?" (Acts 1:6). Luke-Acts is the source of our liturgical practice that clearly differentiates cross, resurrection, ascension, and sending of the Spirit. John, by way of contrast, sees everything happening on the cross. Jesus' crucifixion is his exaltation and the moment when he hands over the Spirit. When Jesus shows the disciples his hands and his side in the resurrection narrative (Jn 20:19–23), he is clearly pointing them to the cross for the proper understanding of both the resurrection and the gift of the Spirit, as the witness at the foot of the cross had already emphasized (19:35). The point is that cross–resurrection–ascension–Pentecost form one single event from a theological perspective. That "event" is an apocalyptic event. It is the final and decisive act of God that embraces and fulfills the whole of human history. As such, it is the revelation of the end of history. Even though history as we know it has continued to the present, God by way of anticipation has revealed in Christ the divine intention for the whole.

In a sense, God can tell us no more about the divine intention than that at the moment of death divine love will embrace us. That transforming embrace of love includes the whole of creation. Jesus is in truth the "firstborn of all creation." The power which Jesus has now is the power of his Spirit. Hence the only possible response to the disciples' question: "But you will receive power when the Holy Spirit has come upon you; and you will be my witnesses in Jerusalem, in all Judea and Samaria, and to the ends of the earth" (Acts 1:8). The risen Jesus lives with God in a transformed and exalted existence. As such, he cannot return to this life as we know it. But he continues to be present in the power of his Spirit. That this is so fits well with the image of God as one who dialogues (see Q. 59). Through the paschal mysteries Jesus has empowered us to respond and to take responsibility until he comes again. We are called to create with him the full and final realization of God's kingdom.

Q. 72. What about the appearances to the disciples? Don't they show that Jesus returned to this life at least for a while?

Here it is helpful to distinguish earlier tradition from later developments. Paul offers one of the earliest formulations, which he says that he himself had received (presumably in Damascus around the time of his conversion some three years after the death of Jesus) at 1 Corinthians 15:3–8. The four essential elements are the simple claims that Christ died, that he was buried, that he was raised, and that he appeared to Cephas. "Buried" confirms "died" in the sense that his death was real. In the same way, "appeared" confirms "raised." Inseparable from the claim that Jesus was raised is the fact that he appeared to Simon Peter. This is the basic proclamation of the early church which is also formulated at Luke 24:34 as follows: ". . . that the Lord has truly been raised and has appeared to Simon" (tr. mine). Whether Peter was chronologically the first or not, he is eventually given a symbolic primacy of place as the "rock" or foundation of Christian faith. In principle only one such revelation was necessary. Paul lists others: the twelve, the more than five hundred, James, all the apostles, and finally himself. But he insists that the experience is essentially the same, for there is only one gospel because there is only one revelation.

Paul is the only apostle to give us a first-hand account of such an experience (Gal 1:6–24). He does not describe the subjective experience in physical terms, as Luke describes Paul's conversion (in three different versions at Acts 9:1–22; 22:3–16; 26:4–18). It probably involved some form of seeing or hearing, but Paul places the emphasis on the divine activity. It was God who "was pleased to reveal his Son to me" (Gal 1:16). He insists that the gospel he proclaims did not come to him through any human mediation but only "through a revelation of Jesus Christ" (1:11–12). It is this revelation that gave him his mission "so that I might proclaim him among the Gentiles" (1:16). Paul insists throughout his career that he too is an apostle because he too has seen Jesus (1 Cor 9:1). The one and unique revelation has produced the one gospel which is the same for all the apostles (Gal 1:6–9; 2:1–10; 1 Cor 15:1–2.11). Thus, the "appearances" mean at the earliest and most fundamental level a revelatory disclosure from God of the presence and significance of Jesus. Since the resurrection itself is an eschatological event signifying the end of history, it is the absolutely unique, once-for-all revelation. There can be no other revelation that is final and definitive in this sense. The revelatory initiative of God calls for a response of faith which includes a being sent on mission to proclaim this good news. This is the apostolic foundation of the church.

Q. 73. Didn't Jesus eat and drink with his disciples after he rose?

This brings us to the later developments of the tradition, and especially to the stories of the appearances. Paul's writings give us the basic claim of the early church that Jesus was raised and appeared to all the apostles from Peter to Paul himself. Though Paul knows that Jesus was buried, he never mentions the empty tomb. This first appears in Mark 16:1–8 (vv. 9–20 are a later addition to the gospel). But in Mark there is no appearance of Jesus. A "young man" (an angel-like revelatory figure) announces to the women the basic proclamation: "He has been raised" (v. 6). The empty tomb now proves to be the occasion for the development of stories about the appearances of Jesus. Matthew 28:1–20 represents something of a transitional stage. He retains and indeed elaborates the revelatory encounter with the angel but then parallels it with a similar appearance of Jesus himself (vv. 9–10). Nonetheless, Matthew's primary focus is upon the instructions of an already exalted Lord to his church for all times until the end of time (vv. 16–20). It is with Luke 24:1–53 that we come closest to imagining the risen Jesus as a resuscitated corpse. He eats with the disciples and allows them to touch him in order to prove that he is not a ghost but really has "flesh and bones." Yet, also in Luke, the primary concern is to communicate the basic proclamation (vv. 5–7.19–20.26.34.46) which is tied closely to the fulfillment of scripture (vv. 25–27.32.44–46). The extremely physical demonstration (vv. 36–43) may be Luke's way of fulfilling Jesus' prediction at the last supper that he will not eat or drink "until it is fulfilled in the kingdom of God" (22:15–18). Finally, John represents something of a challenge to those who insist on physical demonstration in order to believe (doubting Thomas). "Blessed are those who have not seen and yet have come to believe" (Jn 20:29).

All of our sources agree on this fundamental Christian fact: that God has really and truly raised Jesus from the dead. This is the indispensable fact upon which the whole of Christian faith is based. Whether one chooses to believe that Jesus literally appeared to the disciples as narrated in Matthew, Luke, and John or not, one cannot maintain continuity with the apostolic tradition and deny the fact of the resurrection. The stories of the appearances, like the infancy narratives, communicate this central religious truth in the best way possible. Luke's account of the two disciples on the way to Emmaus (24:13–35) is a wonderful story that gives very concrete shape to our image of the risen Jesus. Who is this risen and mysterious figure? He is the same Jesus whom we knew prior to his death: the Jesus who walked with us on the way, explained the scriptures to us, entered our homes and broke bread with us. He is the same Jesus but now transformed by the power of the Spirit. We continue to recognize him in the breaking of the bread.

Q. 74. If the empty tomb isn't even mentioned until Mark's gospel, how important is it? Does it prove that Jesus rose?

In and of itself an empty tomb proves nothing. It is an ambiguous fact awaiting explanation. Did the disciples make a mistake and go to the wrong tomb because he was buried by his enemies (the latter seems to be the natural meaning of Acts 13:29)? Did the disciples steal the body (an accusation already recorded at Mt 28:11–15)? Was Jesus raised from the dead (the Christian claim)? These are all possible explanations. The empty tomb, like the appearance narratives, does not prove the resurrection. Rather, it is resurrection faith that interprets the meaning of the empty tomb. It was perhaps for this reason that it was either presumed and ignored or unknown in Paul's writings. But, given the priority of the revelatory disclosure and the corresponding response of faith, the empty tomb like the narratives does serve to make more concrete our image of the risen Jesus. In this case it confirms the truly "physical" or "bodily" character of the resurrection.

Even though the empty tomb is not mentioned until the writing of Mark around 69 C.E., there seems to be no good reason to doubt an historical core to the tradition. The simplest statement of it is found at John 20:1: "Early on the first day of the week, while it was still dark, Mary Magdalene came to the tomb and saw that the stone had been removed from the tomb." Mary Magdalene is the one person to whom all the traditions point. In her distraught state (Jn 20:2.11–15), she made her way to the tomb, perhaps to give Jesus a proper burial, and found it empty. On the assumption that there was a tomb that was known, could the early church have proclaimed Jesus' resurrection, in the context of how that would be understood in those days, if his body lay in a tomb? It is worth noting that the empty tomb itself was never called into question at that time, only its interpretation (Mt 28:15).

Q. 75. How much does what we know about Jesus depend on the resurrection?

I would say everything we say about Jesus depends on the resurrection. But the resurrection must not be understood as an isolated event unrelated to the cross as specifying that it is the resurrection of this crucified man (see Q. 67). In addition to the cross-resurrection as one inseparable event, we must relate this event to the human and historical life of Jesus that preceded and to the continuing Spirit-filled life of the church that followed. This entire complex constitutes the "Christ-event," i.e. the whole story of Jesus.

What enabled the early church to move from Jesus' own proclamation of the kingdom of God to the proclamation of Jesus himself as Christ and Lord was the revelatory experience of the resurrection. What this experience revealed was not simply that the disciples now knew him in a way they had not known him before, i.e. that their knowledge of him had changed. What this experience revealed was much more basically that Jesus himself was now different, that he had been changed, transformed into the new human being, the Son of Man. Jesus had proclaimed that God would vindicate his ministry, employing the apocalyptic image of the "Day of the Son of Man." His failure and rejection was reversed and transcended by the apocalyptic "event" of the cross-resurrection. The inevitable conclusion flowing from the same Spirit who had anointed and inspired Jesus during his ministry and who had transformed him in the embrace of divine love is that Jesus now *is* the Son of Man. This may well have been the earliest explicit affirmation of his identity using a Christological title that we have.

This affirmation led very quickly to the insight that if he has been identified with the final and decisive act of God's creativity in the resurrection, then he is identified with the whole of God's creative activity. Thus he is seen as the Son of Man who will return soon with great power and glory (Mk 13:24–27); as the Son of Man exalted to the right hand of God (Mk 14:62); as the Son of Man who had authority on earth to forgive sins and to challenge the powers of his day (Mk 2:10.28); as the Son of Man who had to be rejected and killed (Mk 8:31; 9:31; 10:33). Soon other titles came into play to help the church expand and develop her Christological understanding, but all of this development was rooted and grounded in the central and decisive experience of the resurrection. The indispensable catalyst was the inspiration of the Holy Spirit who led the early church into the whole truth about Jesus (Jn 16:12–15).

Q. 76. Are you saying that Jesus became something that he was not before?

No. There was never a time when Jesus was not the Son of Man and the Son of God, the Christ and Lord. There are biblical texts which, if taken in isolation, might seem to indicate the contrary. For example, Peter's speech at Pentecost which proclaims Jesus' resurrection, exaltation, and pouring out of the Spirit concludes: "Therefore let the entire house of Israel know with certainty that God has made him both Lord and Messiah, this Jesus whom you crucified" (Acts 2:36). This sounds as if Jesus was first constituted as such at the resurrection, yet the same author (Luke) has already in the infancy narratives presented Jesus as the Son of God who will occupy the throne of David (Lk 1:32). Two observations are necessary.

First, individual texts can be isolated from their contexts in the NT writings and analyzed for their possible place and significance within the unfolding and diverse dynamic of the early church's evolving Christology. This is a useful and necessary undertaking for specialists who seek to understand more clearly exactly how the church's Christology developed. But even the specialists must eventually reinsert the texts into their contexts and see them as part of the integral theology of the author. Moreover, while respecting the diversity and individuality of the various NT writings, the ultimate goal of such analysis is to find the underlying consistency that justifies such Christological development even in its diversity. I find it in the proclamation that God has raised Jesus from the dead. All subsequent Christological affirmations are an attempt to interpret in varying circumstances the significance of the risen Jesus.

Second, when we call Jesus Lord and Christ, Son of Man and Son of God, we are seeking to express the significance of his life as a whole in the light of resurrection faith. To say that the risen Jesus is now the Son of God is to say that he always was the Son of God whether we push his origins back to his baptism, his conception, or the beginning of creation (see Q. 14). But, on the other hand, we are saying that he is the Son of God by living the kind of human life he actually lived with all the struggles and temptations, joys and sorrows, that he personally experienced. The later Christological affirmations of the church are not intended to deny the full actuality of his human life and experience; they are intended to affirm it. This human life was God's own human life! But this was a human life in which he did grow in wisdom, age, and grace before God and before his people (Lk 2:40.52).

Q. 77. Christology seems very confusing. Why can't we just look on Jesus as a good person, a prophet or a saint, who wanted to bring others to believe more fully in the power of God?

While it is not necessary for everyone to enter into all the intricacies of Christological development, it is important to realize that its origins lie in the concretely lived experience of the early communities. "Jesus is Lord!" is not a theoretical statement. It is one of the earliest creedal statements. It is the experience of Jesus' Spirit active in the midst of the community at worship that gave rise to this basic confession of faith. Whatever attempts we make subsequently to gain theoretical understanding of our faith, we are always driven back to this originating experience in worship. If the inspiration of the Spirit is not seen as the root and ground of Christology, then of course it can seem to be mere verbal game-playing. A valid Christology arises from and returns to the community gathered together and empowered by the Spirit of Jesus.

There are many today, including Christians, who would reduce Jesus to what we know of him historically. Certainly he was a good person, a holy man, a prophet, but he was also more than a prophet (Mt 12:38–42 par.). This is why it is important to see that our scriptures were not written simply from the perspective of historical interest but from the perspective of resurrection faith. That faith is the response to the creative initiative of a God who wills the salvation of all people. In my view, Christology should always be seen as the deepest expression of soteriology, i.e. of God's desire to bring us to the fullness of human liberation. Christology at root expresses God's personal self-involvement in the creative-salvific process of world history. This self-involvement moves progressively and ever more profoundly from creation to covenant to incarnation. What we believe about Jesus is that God has become one of us, like us in all things except sin. Jesus is "the human face of God" (J.A.T. Robinson), "the sacrament of the encounter with God" (E. Schillebeeckx), "the word of life" whom we have heard, whom we have seen with our eyes, whom we have looked at and touched with our hands, who was with the Father and has been revealed to us (1 Jn 1:1–2). Incarnation is not only essential to Christian faith; it is what gives Christian faith its distinctive and radical character.

Q. 78. Why do we call Jesus "God" sometimes and at other times call him the "Son of God"?

Actually the appropriate title for Jesus, and the one that eventually became predominant in the development of NT Christology, is

"Son of God." "God" (*ho theos*) in the NT is reserved almost exclusively for the Father. Even John, who gives us the clearest affirmations of Jesus' divine status, differentiates in the prologue (1:1) between the Word's relation to "the God" (*ho theos*) and the Word as divine (*theos*). The only time Jesus is directly referred to as *ho theos* occurs in Thomas' burst of adoration before the risen Jesus: "My Lord and my God!" (Jn 20:28). When we use the term "God" for Jesus we are reflecting the development of trinitarian faith that includes Father, Son, and Spirit within our conviction, derived from Jewish monotheism, that there is only one God. One of the classic tensions of Christian faith has been to maintain monotheism, that there is only one God, and yet to affirm threeness within that oneness.

Paul gives us an early and interesting text, probably citing a very early creed, within the context of a discussion about idolatry: ". . . yet for us there is one God, the Father, from whom are all things and for whom we exist, and one Lord, Jesus Christ, through whom are all things and through whom we exist" (1 Cor 8:6). Paul is alluding to Israel's central confession of faith: "Hear, O Israel, the LORD is our God, the Lord alone" (Dt 6:4). But he is splitting that confession so that "Lord" refers to Jesus and "God" refers to the Father. God, the Father, is the origin and goal of all things and especially of our existence, but as mediated through Jesus Christ as Lord. Yet, both are called "one"—one God and one Lord. Jesus is always in the bosom of the Father (Jn 1:18), and whatever we say about him as divine can only be said as of the Father's only Son (Jn 1:14). Another early hymn expresses the same idea: ". . . and every tongue should confess that Jesus Christ is Lord, to the glory of God the Father" (Phil 2:11).

Q. 79. Can you say something more about the Trinity? How can God be both one and three?

"No one has ever seen God. It is God the only Son, who is close to the Father's heart, who has made him known" (Jn 1:18). It is far easier to speak of the Trinity in its historical manifestations than to speculate about the inner divine life. As one author put it, anyone who speaks of the Trinity speaks of the cross of Christ and does not speculate in heavenly riddles (J. Moltmann). It is Jesus in his historical life, death, and resurrection who reveals the reality of the triune God. The triune reality is grounded in Jesus' anointing by the Spirit and missioning by the Father at his baptism (Mk 1:9–11). His whole human life was one of obedient response to the Father's will in the power of the Spirit. That relationship culminated with his handing over of the Spirit to the Father on the cross and with the Father's embracing him, lifting him up and transforming him, in that same Spirit. John has seen clearly that this mutual self-giving breaks the bonds of human limitation and signifies an eternal relationship of love. Thus Jesus prays: "I glorified you on earth by finishing the work that you gave me to do. So now, Father, glorify me in your own presence with the glory that I had in your presence before the world existed" (Jn 17:4–5).

Later creeds and councils have simply sought to affirm this biblical affirmation of Jesus' eternal relation to the Father in the unity of the Spirit. They affirm that the revelation given in Jesus communicates the truth about the reality of God. They do not attempt to explain *how* this is so, although many theologians, such as St. Augustine in his *De Trinitate,* have sought to explore the ways in which such a mystery might be more intelligible to us. For me, the most important and fundamental insight is this: at the very heart of reality, at the very center of all that is, i.e. in the lived reality of the living God who is Creator of all, there is *relationship.* God does not live in splendid isolation, an unmoved mover that draws all to itself but gives nothing in return, an indifferent and apathetic being far removed from and untouched by our pain. Rather, God is *personal* who as Father communicates all of the divine life to the Son and still remains Father. The Son in turn is the image of the invisible God (Col 1:15) who eternally reflects the glory of the Father and makes him known to us (Jn 1:14.18). The bonding of this relationship from Father to Son, the Father as source and origin who initiates the relationship and the Son as response and image who reflects the

Father's glory, is the Holy Spirit. This is where we come in. Do we not see here the meaning of our loves, whether our love be the creative love of parents (*eros*), the mutually empowering love of friends (*philia*), or the self-giving love of Jesus (*agape:* see Jn 15:12–17)?

Q. 80. When Jesus was on earth, was he still a part of the Trinity or was it only when he was raised from the dead?

The problem facing the post-biblical fathers and councils was how to interpret the biblical data to a Greek culture with its particular linguistic and philosophical orientation. The gospel of John was the focus of interest because the prologue speaks of the Word (*Logos*) which had special connotations in Greek philosophy and because the rest of the gospel is built on Jesus' eternal relation to the Father. But John's gospel does not address the later Greek problem of how the Word can be divine (Jn 1:1) and still become flesh (Jn 1:14). It simply assumes that what has been said of Jesus *in the light of the resurrection,* namely that he is the Son of God, means that he always was the Son of God even before the foundation of the world. There is a kind of poetic innocence here, for John is only concerned to proclaim the significance of Jesus for the whole of creation.

But when we use the name "Jesus," do we mean the human, historical Jesus who was born at a particular time, lived, and died? Or perhaps we mean that he existed as the primal Man before all other creatures (a possible interpretation of John). In the light of the Arian controversy (see Q. 15), the Council of Nicea in 325 essentially differentiated Jesus' eternal begetting from the Father as the *Logos* (the response and image of the Father) and his descending and becoming incarnated in time for us and for our salvation. Yet, to say this the council employs the biblical titles "one Lord, Jesus Christ, the Son of God" and does not employ the word *Logos.* This indicates that the council's affirmations, like the entire development of Christology, are based on the biblical witness to the resurrection.

By effectively separating Jesus' eternal relation to the Father from his appearance in time, the council took the fateful step of separating his divinity from his humanity (something I do not think that John does even with his language of descent and ascent). It was now possible to think of Jesus as God who subsequently took on our flesh (became incarnate). But this separates precisely what needs to be kept together. Whatever significance we attach to the name "Jesus," which is the central symbol of Christian faith, we cannot understand who he is apart from his humanness. So far as we know, in the light of the resurrection, he does not exist as a human being apart from the divinity that makes him uniquely who he is nor as a divine being apart from the humanity that allows him to know and love the Father and to pray to him as *Abba*. God as Creator—imaged as Father, as Word, as Spirit—has come to final and definitive self-expression in the Son who, as risen, is a life-giving Spirit (1 Cor 15:45). Jesus has always been, inseparably and eternally, "part" of the Trinity.

Q. 81. You constantly refer to the Bible in your explanations. But hasn't the church in the councils settled all these questions?

Karl Rahner was once asked whether the Council of Chalcedon in 451 was an end or a beginning. He said it was both. It brought a certain discussion among the Greek fathers to a conclusion, but it also opened up all kinds of questions which future generations have tried to address. Your question gives me the opportunity to re-emphasize a point made earlier: our attempts to understand the mystery of Jesus involve a continuing process of interpretation. Insofar as we are attempting to bring to expression the mystery of the "God for us" (C. LaCugna), no answer can be considered final. Unless we revert to fundamentalism, neither the Bible, nor the creeds and councils, nor the writings of theologians and bishops, nor any human statement whatsoever will exhaust this mystery.

The wonder of Christian faith is that we celebrate the wedding of heaven and earth. We believe in a God for us, a God who has come as close as divinely possible to us in the humanness of his Son.

We believe in a God who is not in competition with us but who works in and through us for the full liberation of humanity. "Jesus' divinity is his humanness to the utmost" (P. Schoonenberg). What we say of him as divine does not erase his humanness; it brings the human to unique fulfillment.

The first two ecumenical councils were concerned to affirm the full divinity of the Son (Nicea in 325) and the full divinity of the Spirit (Constantinople I in 381). The latter, in rejecting the position of Apollinaris that the Word (*Logos*) had replaced the human soul in Jesus, also affirmed his full humanity. But the crucial issue was the oneness of Jesus. Cyril of Alexandria and the Council of Ephesus in 431 affirm that Jesus is one uniquely existent individual (a "unity according to hypostasis" which is what was later meant by the unity of one "person"). It is hard to overemphasize the importance of this. It means that Jesus' divinity and humanity, however distinct, are *inseparable* in him. He is not first God and then a human being. The concretely existent reality of Jesus, what makes him unique *as human,* is union with the divine. Finally, the Council of Chalcedon in 451, in the light of this strong sense of inseparable unity, had to maintain the distinct and irreducible nature of both humanity and divinity. The humanity is not overwhelmed by the divinity and absorbed into it. Rather, the divinity is what enables or empowers the humanity to be fully itself, like us in all things except sin (Heb 4:15, cited in the definition of Chalcedon). In all this, the fathers and councils had but one purpose: to remain faithful to the apostolic tradition, the "rule of faith" which is contained primarily in the canon of scripture. I seek to do the same, but in the light of contemporary advances in biblical criticism.

Q. 82. How could Jesus have been 100% human and at the same time 100% divine? Isn't that 200%?

One of the most unfortunate impressions created by the Council of Chalcedon gives rise to precisely this kind of question. The language of Chalcedon, influenced by Pope Leo the Great, is very

Roman in its desire for balance. While repeating eight times that we confess "one and the same" Son, Jesus Christ, our Lord, the key is the application of *homoousios* (see Q. 15) to both divinity and humanity. He is said to be of the "same being" as the Father in his divinity and of the "same being" as us in his humanity. In insisting upon the irreducible and distinct character of the two natures, preserving the properties appropriate to each, the council creates the impression of a rather static juxtaposition of two entities so that the language of union remains ambiguous: "flowing together [*suntrechousēs* = 'running together'] into one person (*prosopon*) and one subsistence (*hypostasis*)." The most widespread and common reaction to Chalcedon at the time was to return to the monophysite position, i.e. that by reason of the union the humanity was absorbed into the divinity so that there is only "one nature," the divine. To some degree this has been the popular image even to modern times. Jesus is really God who uses his human nature to communicate with us, but his humanness is more a way of appearing than integral to the concretely lived experience of Jesus himself.

The great value of Chalcedon is its insistence upon the fullness of Jesus' humanity. With all the councils, we maintain the fullness of divinity and the fullness of humanity within the unity of one "person." However, what must be remembered is that divinity and humanity are incommensurable realities. You cannot balance them as if they were two measurable and comparable quantities. The divine is not in competition with the human nor should it be set over against the human. Apart from the divinity, we cannot speak properly of the reality of Jesus. He is constituted uniquely as this man Jesus by reason of his union with the divine. On the other hand, we cannot speak properly of his personality apart from the humanity. He is presented in scripture as one who knows and loves the Father and who prays to him as "I" to "Thou." He is obedient even to death. These are all ways we expect a normal human person to act. Thus, the use of the word "person" shifts depending upon whether we are speaking of that which constitutes him as a uniquely existent individual (*hypostasis*) or that which constitutes his normal human experiences of knowing and willing ("person" in the contemporary sense of human relationships on the psychological level). In this latter sense, it is proper to call him a human person.

Q. 83. You have said a number of times that the divine is not in competition with the human. What do you mean?

This is of a piece with what I have said earlier about the "God who dialogues" (see QQ. 59–61). God's intention is to realize the fullness of what it is to be human from within human life and experience. God's presence and activity in creation, in covenant with Israel, in becoming incarnate in Jesus, is not intended to alienate us from our humanness. The world is not just an effect of God's causality as if it existed apart from or parallel to or in competition with God. The world is the embodiment of the divine intention, just as a work of art embodies the artist. The work is distinct from the artist, but surely the artist is not indifferent to what happens to it. The work expresses the artist's very self, the way the artist views the world and imagines it taking shape. The work also expresses the limitations of the medium chosen. One thinks of Michelangelo taking a piece of Carrara marble that no one else wanted because it had a fissure down the middle and creating his greatest masterpiece, the statue of David. Once a medium is chosen, an artist must work within its limitations but also make positive use of them to exploit the possibilities of the medium to the *full*. The capacity to do so is what marks a great artist.

So it is with the incarnation. We should not imagine it as a divine "self-emptying" (*kenosis*), a withdrawal or hiding of the divinity in order to allow the humanity to go into action, but a divine "filling" (*plēroma:* Col 1:19; 2:9—the latter speaks of the "whole fullness" of God dwelling in Jesus). Even in the humanness of Jesus as the incarnation of God, God can communicate the divine self only to the degree that the created human reality is able to receive the divine self-communication. What we see in salvation history is the progressive and deepening communication and involvement of God from creation through covenant to incarnation. In Jesus God brings to fullness or completion the work begun, the creation of the "human being." God does this by working with the limitations and possibilities of this particular human life, Jesus of Nazareth, calling forth the full and faithful response of human obedience and in the climactic event of death-resurrection transforming the separation of sin into the grace of union, the weakness of flesh into the integrity of glory, and the mortal power of death into eternal life. By this we know that the "Son of Man" is the "Son of God."

Q. 84. Returning to scripture, if the Jesus of Mark's gospel is so different from the Jesus of John's gospel, how do you reconcile them?

The concern of the fathers and councils, of course, was to bring to expression in an official and universal formulation the unity of faith. The Nicene Creed that we recite in church on Sundays (but which comes from the First Council of Constantinople in 381) was formulated not so much to resolve theological riddles as to provide a communal foundation for liturgical prayer. The important issue, then and now, is how we pray together, not whether we all think the same thoughts or have uniform understandings. How can we pray to Jesus as God if he is not God? Yet even that affirmation of Nicea concerning Jesus' divinity is open to multiple interpretations.

The creedal unity of faith is grounded in the biblical witness. Yet it is to the credit of the early church as it formed its canon of scriptures that the desire for unity did not lead to the suppression of all the gospels but one. The various letters of Paul and others as well as the four gospels offer quite diverse and distinctive portraits of Jesus. Matthew and Luke, even though they use Mark, have their own quite distinctive Christologies. The first order of business is to allow each portrait to stand on its own terms and not try to collapse them into one, such as the harmonizing approach to the "Lives of Christ," e.g. Alban Goodier, tried to do in the past (see Q. 7).

It is important, then, to read Mark and John as they were written, to try to understand them as distinct expressions of the one Christian faith by quite different communities. Both seek to proclaim the mystery of Jesus, but the pattern of each is different. Some authors have characterized the difference as reflecting Christologies "from below" (Jesus as the man anointed by God's Spirit who became God's Son) and "from above" (Jesus as the eternal Word of God who became incarnate in human form). However, I think such a contrast reflects later theological developments and does not in this form correspond to any of the biblical Christologies. For both Mark and John, Jesus is inseparably the "Son of God" and the "Son of Man" from the beginning of the story to the end. What might be said is that the synoptics (Mark–Matthew–Luke) incorporate more of the historical memory of Jesus, of what he actually said and did, whereas John incorporates more of the community's later faith experience of him, especially of his eternal uniqueness as God's only Son. But even this can be overdrawn. All the gospels tell the same story, but from different perspectives and with different interests arising from each one's contemporary situation when writing the gospel. The story of Jesus has at least as many forms as there are Christian communities that bear witness to him—and they are all true.

Q. 85. Is Jesus still present in the world today?

Both the scriptures and continuing Christian tradition would say, most emphatically, yes! Matthew ends his gospel where he began, with Jesus as Emmanuel (God with us): "And remember, I am with you always, to the end of the age" (Mt 28:20). For Luke in Acts, Jesus continues to live in the gift of the Holy Spirit which he has poured out (Acts 2:33). Yet it is still Jesus whom Paul is persecuting (9:3–5). Likewise, in John, Jesus promises that the dwelling place he is preparing is in the heart of those who love him and keep his commandments. It is there that the Father and he will dwell (Jn 14:23). In addition, he promises the help of the Holy Spirit who will lead the disciples into all truth, declaring what belongs jointly to Jesus and to the Father (Jn 16:12–15). Paul puts it this way: "For in the one Spirit we were all baptized into one body—Jews or Greeks, slaves or free—and we were all made to drink of one Spirit" (1 Cor 12:13).

We can say that Jesus is present in three "bodily" ways. First, as risen Lord he is present to the whole cosmos (see Q. 70). Second, through baptism he is present to the whole Christian community and to each member who collectively and individually constitutes his body. "Now you are the body of Christ and individually members of it" (1 Cor 12:27). Third, in the eucharistic celebration he is present in a unique way under the physical appearance of bread and wine (see Q. 45). The eucharist might be compared to a birthday party. We celebrate the presence of a person who is always with us but whose life, both past and future, we wish to affirm and proclaim through special symbolic actions and words. "For as often as you eat this bread and drink this cup, you proclaim the Lord's death until he comes" (1 Cor 11:26).

Q. 86. Has the Spirit of Jesus shaped human lives everywhere and at all times?

The Spirit of Jesus is the Spirit of God, what we call the Holy Spirit, recognized officially at the First Council of Constantinople in 381 as the third person of the Trinity who equally and together with the Father and the Son is adored and glorified. St. Augustine has called the Holy Spirit the love between the Father and the Son. While not quite making that identification, Paul says: ". . . God's love has been poured into our hearts through the Holy Spirit that has been given to us" (Rom 5:5). God who is love (1 Jn 4:8.16) is inseparably and eternally the living and loving relationship we call Father–Son–Spirit.

There are three Greek words for love that capture well the activity of God's Spirit in human lives. First, *eros* is the kind of creative love that a man and a woman have in the begetting of children. God's creative love is expressed as the Spirit or Breath (*ruah*) of God who hovers over the waters (Gen 1:2) and breathes the breath of life into the human creature (Gen 2:7). It is the same creative Spirit who comes upon Mary (Lk 1:35). Second, *philia* is the love of friendship. God's covenantal love moves beyond creativity to mutual empowerment. "I will be your God and you will be my people" means that God makes a commitment to us and expects a response in kind. Jesus speaks of such love: ". . . I have called you friends, because I have made known to you everything that I have heard from my Father" (Jn 15:15b). According to John, God in Jesus wishes to communicate the deepest and most intimate mystery of the divine reality. That is what friends do. Third, *agape* is the love that gives even one's very life for the good of the beloved. "No one has greater love than this, to lay down one's life for one's friends" (Jn 15:13). And indeed: "God's love was revealed among us in this way: God sent his only Son into the world so that we might live through him" (1 Jn 4:9). Hence we can say: were it not for God's Spirit, that is, God's creative, covenantal, and self-giving love, there would be no human life anywhere or at any time.

Q. 87. Why is it often said that Jesus or his Spirit lives in everyone when there are so many ruthless murderers and criminals in the world? Is Jesus part of them?

The love of God in Christ Jesus our Lord excludes no one. According to Paul, we have all sinned and fallen short of God's glory (Rom 3:23), but while we were still sinners and enemies of God, God has proven his love for us in Jesus' death on the cross for our sakes (Rom 5:8). Jesus' challenge to those who would stone the woman caught in adultery remains in force: "Let anyone among you who is without sin be the first to throw a stone at her" (Jn 8:7).

The question is really one of forgiveness (see Q. 49). In the final analysis, the only unforgivable sin is human hardness of heart, i.e. the refusal to accept forgiveness and to forgive others. Jesus' death on the cross is the ultimate embrace of one's enemies in love and forgiveness. Personally, I oppose capital punishment because too frequently it is an act of revenge, a refusal to forgive. Moreover, such an act effectively refuses to believe that this particular person is redeemable, that he or she can have a conversion of mind and heart and begin to lead a new life. Capital punishment is only punitive; it has given up on rehabilitation. Jesus never gave up on anyone, not even his most obstinate enemies.

The question is how deeply we are willing and able to forgive. The parable of the unmerciful servant (Mt 18:23–35), as Matthew gives it to us, makes the final point in v. 35 that God's forgiveness cannot be effective in our lives if we do not forgive our brothers and sisters from the heart. The focus is on the judgment of the king

(= God). This is true, but if we take the story on its own terms without the final application of v. 35, the surprising turn comes at the moment when the king goes back on his word and reverses his earlier forgiveness. A king's honor would require him to keep his word (cp. Herod at Mk 6:26). Not only that, but he now condemns the servant to unending torture, a far worse punishment than the one ordered previously (v. 25). The fellow servants' action in reporting all to the king rather than seeking another way of forgiveness and reconciliation had consequences far beyond what they intended. The point is this: as we hear the parable, can we forgive even a fellow servant who is as crass and unmerciful as this one? How deeply are we willing to forgive and to seek other ways than violence and revenge to resolve conflicts? "Indeed God did not send the Son into the world to condemn the world, but in order that the world might be saved through him" (Jn 3:17).

Q. 88. What about people of other religions, like Hindus or Buddhists, or even atheists? Does Jesus make a difference to them?

Yes, if what we said earlier about the resurrection (see QQ. 68–70) is true. The risen Jesus embodies God's intention for the fullness of human life and experience. Moreover, the significance of the resurrection extends to the whole of creation. Our Christian hope is that all things will be transformed in Christ. Yet we are still in the process of discerning the concrete and specific ways that will lead to this final transformation. In this process we can learn from other religious traditions as they can learn from us. Mutually empowering dialogue is absolutely necessary. We must honestly and openly recognize what unites us as well as what divides us.

All religions, as well as humanistic atheists, converge in a universal care and concern for creation, for the earth, for her well-being and destiny. An instinct that is truly religious (and so truly human) can never be indifferent to mother earth and her many children who pulsate and interact as a mysterious whole. Moreover, religions tend to have much more in common on the levels of ethical concern (action) and mystical prayer (contemplation). They divide more readily over doctrines or the formulations of their fundamental beliefs. These latter suffer from the limitations of human beings trying to express the absolutely transcendent. But it is precisely here that we have much to learn from one another. Jesus as risen transcends all religions, including Christianity. We Christians bring to the discussion profound convictions about the central significance of Jesus for all humankind. We cease to be Christian if we do not proclaim him as the very incarnation of God.

But we bring these convictions couched in a tradition rooted in the Jewishness of Jesus but very quickly expressing itself in Greek (eastern) and Latin (western) terms. The Roman Catholic Church is basically western European in its cultural and religious expression, although it is becoming more and more a world church. All Christians (Roman, Orthodox, Protestant) must learn to listen to the voices of Asia, Africa, and elsewhere if we are to understand the full significance of the resurrection. Jesus does not belong to Christianity; he belongs to all people and the whole of creation. We Christians are called only to bear witness to the truth that is in us, making that truth and way and life (Jn 14:6) available for all peoples.

Q. 89. Will they all go to heaven, even those who have never heard of Jesus? Isn't baptism essential if we are to be saved?

At the heart of the NT is the urgent command to go forth and proclaim the good news. This is the most fundamental and essential mission of the church. Paul says: ". . . if you confess with your lips that Jesus is Lord and believe in your heart that God raised him from the dead, you will be saved" (Rom 10:9). This leads into an exhortation to go forth and proclaim the good news. Similarly, Peter proclaims in Acts 4:12: "There is salvation in no one else, for there is no other name under heaven given among mortals by which we must be saved." These are two of the more striking texts among many that seem to require explicit faith in Jesus Christ for salvation. Such faith leads to baptism as the sacramental inclusion in the community of the saved. In time this led to the belief that there is no salvation outside the church. There are those who still maintain this, but a rigid interpretation of it broke down long ago with the recognition of "baptism of blood" (martyrdom) and "baptism of desire" (good conscience).

What has happened? First of all, perhaps the most fundamental affirmation of Christian faith is that God wills the salvation of all people (1 Tim 2:4–6; see Q. 61). Jesus himself excluded no one from the kingdom of God. Whatever is said of him subsequently cannot deny this fundamental truth. Second, the writings of the NT reflect the enthusiastic expectation that the gospel would be preached to the ends of the earth (Acts 1:8; 28:30) and that the end would come soon. We can read the texts cited above in a positive way as affirming salvation in Christ without drawing the negative conclusion that those who have not heard of Christ will not be saved. Third, we in the twentieth century are much more acutely aware of the diversity and complexity of human history. This reality conditions our interpretation of the biblical texts. Would we want to believe that the God revealed in Jesus arbitrarily excludes the innumerable people who through no fault of their own have never heard of Jesus? The final state of each human person is known to God alone and should be left to God's judgment. The community of disciples we call church can once again only bear witness through personal and public commitment to the way of life that Jesus has revealed to us.

Q. 90. Why didn't Jesus simply destroy evil once and for all and establish the kingdom on earth?

This question expresses what was probably the hope of many of Jesus' contemporaries (see Q. 33). We have already indicated a number of times that the "God who dialogues" does not act in a coercive manner. Neither the apocalyptic hope of a cataclysmic destruction of this present "evil age" nor the nationalistic hope of triumph over one's enemies corresponds to the way of Jesus Christ. The only question that can be asked fruitfully is not what God might have done but what God has done in Jesus. Matthew recognizes the problem of divine inaction at the arrest of Jesus when one of Jesus' disciples cut off the ear of the high priest's slave: "Put your sword back into its place; for all who take the sword will perish by the

sword. Do you think that I cannot appeal to my Father, and he will
at once send me more than twelve legions of angels?" (Mt 26:52–
53). According to all the gospels, what is happening is in fulfillment
of the scriptures, i.e. the divine will. Luke also adds: "But this is your
hour and the power of darkness!" (Lk 22:53b). God has created us as
creatures of time and space. The divine will is that we take time and
have space to learn the one thing necessary: how to love one another
as Jesus has loved us (Jn 15:12–17). The only divine power that
Jesus has to offer us is the power of love, his Spirit.

However, the question also expresses the deepest desire of every
human heart: that justice be done. This is not the same as revenge or
triumph over one's enemies. Those who "hunger and thirst for righteousness" (Mt 5:6) hunger and thirst for God who is the only truly
just one. The "right" relationship with God is what makes possible
right relationships with one another and with the whole of creation.
In Jesus, God has established just such a relationship and so has
destroyed evil once and for all. "He entered once for all into the
Holy Place, not with the blood of goats and calves, but with his own
blood, thus obtaining eternal redemption" (Heb 9:12). What has
been realized in Jesus is still to be realized in us, and so he has given
us his Spirit and his Word to bring us to justice and judgment:
"Indeed, the word of God is living and active, sharper than any
two-edged sword, piercing until it divides soul from spirit, joints
from marrow; it is able to judge the thoughts and intentions of the
heart. And before him no creature is hidden, but all are naked and
laid bare to the eyes of the one to whom we must render an account"
(Heb 4:12–13).

Q. 91. How do I know if Jesus is listening to me? Why is there so much pain in my life if Jesus loves me so much?

We suggested earlier (see Q. 65) that there is no answer to the
question "why?" when one is confronted with a personal experience
of evil. At one level we must simply accept the fact that each of us is
an integral part of a mysterious and complex universe which continually undergoes processes of change, both growth and decay. We are
born and we die. During our lives we are frequently confronted with

forces beyond our control. Essential to any relationship with God is a simple acceptance of our mortality. The great heresy of our culture, which has also created immeasurable psychological damage, is the denial of death. Not to accept the normal processes of life and death is to be alienated from nature and so from our very selves as embodied creatures.

However, at another level, we are not mere passive sufferers in an unfeeling world. God has endowed us with intellect and will, the capacity to imagine new possibilities and to create them as realities. God is always present in our creativity, for God creates through us. There is no question that God is alive, active, present in our lives, including our pain. The Father knows what we need even before we ask (Mt 6:32). The Son is always listening and attentive, for he has walked the same paths and knows what we feel (Heb 4:15). The Spirit is encouraging and guiding us toward the fullness of love as creative, covenantal, and self-giving. When we pray, then, we do not pray in order to get God's attention. Rather we pray in order that we might be able to hear what God is saying to us. This is one of the things God is saying to us over and over: ". . . I will come again and will take you to myself, so that where I am, there you may be also" (Jn 14:3bc).

Q. 92. In our prayer must we always go to the Father through Jesus or can we pray directly to the Father?

Christian prayer should always be trinitarian. It is Jesus who has revealed to us the threefold nature of the one God. I find the Orthodox tradition of praying to the Father through the Son in the Spirit to have the most solid biblical foundation. This does not mean that we cannot, depending on each one's personal preference, pray now to the Father, now to the Son, and now to the Spirit. But such prayer can never forget that the three are inseparably united in the one divine life. John's gospel is especially strong: "The Father and I are one" (10:30). "Whoever has seen me has seen the Father. . . . Do you not believe that I am in the Father and the Father is in me?" (14:9b.10a)

The last supper discourses in John (chapters 13–17) focus on

the interplay within God of Father, Son, and Spirit and on the mutual indwelling of this same trinitarian life in us and of us in the
trinitarian life. The Trinity is later imaged in the Orthodox tradition
as dancing in a circle. We are invited into the dance, into the dynamic and mutual embrace of love that is God's life. God invites us
in and so "divinizes" us, i.e. makes God's life our own. God invites
us in not to absorb us into the divine life but to transform us by the
power of creative, covenantal, and self-giving love so that we may
come to the fullness of who we are as human persons. God affirms
our personal identity, dignity, and integrity. God wishes us to be
human persons made fully alive, to paraphrase the beautiful insight
of St. Irenaeus. God's gift to us is the Holy Spirit (Lk 11:13). Whatever else we may need or may wish to pray for, this finally is the one
indispensable gift that we pray for. We ask the Father through the
Son to give us the Spirit. With that Spirit, even now, we walk in the
newness of life (Rom 6:4) as a new creation (Gal 6:15; 2 Cor 5:17).
"And this is eternal life, that they may know you, the only true God,
and Jesus Christ whom you have sent" (Jn 17:3). Eternal life has
already begun as we are caught up through faith and prayer into the
trinitarian life of God.

Q. 93. How do I know what God's will is for me?

In Matthew's version of the Lord's Prayer, Jesus tells us to pray:
"Your will be done, on earth as it is in heaven" (6:10b). Jesus himself (but only in Matthew) repeats the exact same words in Gethsemane: "My Father, if this cannot pass unless I drink it, *your will be
done*" (26:42b). For Matthew, Jesus is not only the Wisdom of God
who proclaims and teaches God's will; he embodies it from his baptism in water to his baptism in blood. As a Christian, I can only
know God's will if I receive the gift of his Spirit in baptism and seek
to embody that Spirit by following Jesus on the way in the concrete
and specific conditions of my own life. Seeking to imitate Jesus'
actions in a literal-minded way is foolish and superficial. I must
catch his Spirit and let that Spirit live anew within the context of my
own unique life situation.

Three things should be said about God's will. First, God's will is ultimately a mystery hidden in the intention and power of God. Even Jesus had to seek and discover that will through the concrete experiences of his own life. He was not totally sure of it even toward the end of his life, as the scene in the garden indicates, but he was absolutely sure that he could trust that will "to fulfill all righteousness" (Mt 3:15c). Second, God's intention is revealed in the resurrection. What God wants for the whole of creation and for each human person is the fullness of life, that we each become fully who we are through union with the divine life itself. Third, God has created each person as a unique gift from the hand of God. Each of us must discover how God's intention is to be lived concretely and specifically. Here we need to discern the spirits: to embrace God's Spirit and to drive out the evil spirit. "This kind can come out only through prayer" (Mk 9:29b). The purpose of the *Spiritual Exercises* of St. Ignatius is to immerse us so deeply in the Spirit of God that all other things on the face of the earth can only be understood and evaluated in the light of that Spirit. Knowing God's will is a process of discernment that lasts until death. But one thing is clear. God always asks of us what he asked of Jesus: that we remain faithful to the authentic choices that we have made.

Q. 94. Just how free does God want us to be? Isn't there too much emphasis today on doing whatever I want?

In our American culture freedom is often coupled with rampant individualism, and this is unfortunate. True freedom is not self-centered, does not focus only on my individual rights and choices to the exclusion of the rights and needs of others. Nor is it sufficient to say that I recognize the same for other individuals. This leads to a notion of society as merely a contract that maximizes individual freedom and minimizes social obligation. It is to ignore the fact that, as children of the one God who has created us, we do belong to one another. True freedom, such as exists in God's own trinitarian life, is always relational. None of us is free if any one of our brothers or sisters is enslaved.

The contemporary movement known as "liberation theology," which began in the 1960s in Latin America, is concerned to emphasize the intimate connection between our Christian faith and the social, political, and economic realities of our day. Liberation theology does not claim to be a new theology among others, but *the way* to do theology. The primary appeal is to scripture. Thus the exodus experience becomes a central focus because it expresses three indispensable elements: freedom from past oppression (enslavement in Egypt); taking present responsibility as a newly established community for our relationships to God and to one another (covenant expressed principally in the ten commandments); freedom for the future as God's future (a community of hope symbolized by the land as the fulfillment of God's promises).

The history of Israel is the history of a people struggling to remain faithful to God and to one another. The prophets are particularly critical of failures in social responsibility: to the poor, the widow, the orphan, the stranger as symbolizing the most vulnerable and oppressed. They symbolize Israel's failure to live up to the covenant. To oppress the poor is to deny the God of Israel. Jesus comes from within that tradition and proclaims that God's kingdom is arriving particularly for the poor and oppressed (see QQ. 32–33). Individualistic interpretations of scripture that ignore the social concerns of Moses and Jesus are convenient for those who wish to maintain the status quo of poverty and oppression, but they also deny "the freedom of the glory of the children of God" (Rom 8:21b). Thus, freedom is not a license to do whatever I want. Freedom is a glorious responsibility to care for and nourish others, and especially the poor, the marginated, the humiliated and despised in our midst. If we did this, we would no longer have to worry so much about protecting our "freedoms."

Q. 95. We hear a lot about women's issues today. Is feminism Christian?

There are varieties of feminism, and so one must be careful in the use of categories. There are some feminists who reject Christianity as hopelessly patriarchal and anti-woman. There are others who feel Christianity has within it the seeds of its own redemption from patriarchy and anti-female bias. I would count myself among the latter. If a feminist is someone, whether man or woman, who believes in the full equality of women and men and who works to make that equality a reality in all social structures, whether civil or religious, then I would call myself a feminist. The question is one of full humanity, and, as I have frequently emphasized before, nothing human can be foreign to an authentic Christianity.

In the sense described, although the term itself is anachronistic, I would say that Jesus by his words and deeds showed himself to be a true feminist. Jesus was concerned with the social oppression of women (see Q. 25). He had very positive views of women and engaged them publicly, even inviting some to be his disciples (see Q. 50). He employed maternal imagery for the God whom he called *Abba* (see Q. 36). In all of this he was strikingly original for his times. With surprising freedom he challenged the deeply entrenched patriarchal structures and practices that were oppressive to women. He offered the vision of a new community, a new way of relating that transcended the divisions and oppressions of rich and poor, slave and free, male and female.

Paul, citing an early baptismal formula, shows that the first Christians understood this: "There is no longer Jew or Greek, there is no longer slave or free, there is no longer male and female; for all of you are one in Christ Jesus" (Gal 3:28). Divisions based on race, class, or sex have been transcended in our oneness in Christ through baptism. Tragically such divisions returned to plague Christianity from early times to the present day. There is no one so oppressed as a poor woman of color. She is oppressed by reason of her class, her sex, and her race. If she is not free, no one of us is free. Is feminism Christian? I would submit that we are not Christian if we are not feminist in the same way as Jesus, i.e. if we do not truly believe in the full equality of women and men and if we do not do all we can to make that equality a reality in our contemporary society.

Q. 96. Why are there so many divisions within Christianity?

As with the different views of Jesus, there is certainly room within Christianity for a legitimate pluralism (see Q. 7). However, there is a difference between a healthy pluralism and irreconcilable differences. Already from the very beginning in biblical times there were different communities with diverse cultural, linguistic, and theological perspectives. At the same time one sees the early church struggling with the question of self-definition, i.e. what unites us as a community of faith and what separates or cuts someone off from that community. Paul says emphatically: "As we have said before, so now I repeat, if anyone proclaims to you a gospel contrary to what you received, let that one be accursed!" (Gal 1:9). The author of the first letter of John, trying to save the gospel of John for the orthodox church, calls the community to "test the spirits to see whether they are from God. . . . By this you know the Spirit of God: every spirit that confesses that Jesus Christ has come in the flesh is from God, and every spirit that does not confess Jesus is not from God" (1 Jn 4:1–3). Matthew affirms the power of the community of faith to bind and to loose in both doctrinal (16:19) and disciplinary (18:18) matters.

Communal interpretation of the faith is an ongoing process as the whole history of Christianity attests. Tragically, often more for political and economic reasons than for strictly theological ones, shattering divisions have occurred. The principal ones have been between the Eastern Orthodox and the Roman Catholics in 1054 and between the Roman Catholics and the Protestants in 1517. The Second Vatican Council (1962–1965) finally recognized that we have all sinned and fallen short of the glory of God, that we must seek anew the unity of all Christians for which Jesus prayed (Jn 17:20–21). The task of ecumenism is not to pretend this history never happened and to hope simplistically that we can return to some earlier golden age. All Christians must recognize and respect the particular history and tradition of each denomination. At the same time we must overcome past divisiveness (often based on prejudices that were emotional and rhetorical rather than factual) and seek that higher unity in Christ Jesus that we have by reason of our baptism (Gal 3:28).

Q. 97. We live in a modern, scientific world. Does Jesus have anything to say to our scientific age?

Science seeks to explain our physical universe through hypothetical models and, if it is practical, to apply that knowledge in a way that can harness the energies and powers of matter for the benefit of human beings. The benefits of science are enormous, and religion can only applaud the creative genius of scientists as a gift from God. In spite of past conflicts, based often on ignorance and fear, there should be no rivalry between science and religion. They simply move on different levels, but both are intended to make the world more human.

A convergent concern of both science and religion today is ecology. To image the earth as mother and the sky as father is religious metaphor that may or may not be appealing to the modern mind. But scientists today, unlike the mechanical view of the universe proposed by Newton, recognize more and more that the universe is a living and vibrant organism in which every part is interconnected and so influences and is influenced by every other part. Feminism and ecology, both coming out of religious concerns, emphasize the connectedness, the relationships, the nurturing care and concern for the other, the sense of social responsibility that increasingly characterize our times.

Jesus was a man of his times and so limited by the scientific knowledge of his day. But he did bring into human consciousness an awareness of divine mystery at the very center of things, a divine mystery that is relational and loving, affirming and enlivening without being competitive or coercive. What Jesus has to say to science is just that: do not be an agent of alienation, domination, coercion, and competition. Such an approach may give you short-term victories in the art of manipulation but it will never lead you into an understanding and appreciation of the mystery that is our physical universe.

Q. 98. Every Sunday we say: "We look for the resurrection of the dead and the life of the world to come." What does that mean?

This phrase is from the "Nicene Creed" which was actually formulated at the First Council of Constantinople in 381. The council is employing the biblical language of apocalyptic. The resurrection of Jesus was an apocalyptic event (see Q. 71). As such it signifies the end of history and final judgment; yet history has continued.

The Pharisees, among others, shared some sort of expectation of a general resurrection at the end of time. What is unique to Christian faith is the claim that this man Jesus has already been raised by way of anticipation of the final end. In Jesus the divine intention has been revealed, yet our hope is that we too shall be raised in him (Rom 6:5–11). Thus "the resurrection of the dead" as the final transformation of all things in Christ is still to come. Embracing the whole of history, it will truly be the end of history as we know it.

It should be noted that this transformation extends to the whole of creation. As J. Moltmann has pointed out, not only human history but evolution as well has had its victims. This means that the coming of Christ at the end of time will signify the redemption not only of humans but of evolution as well. This is why the metaphor of resurrection is so important. The image reaches out to embrace the whole of the physical universe in all its manifestations, from the simplest stones to the most subtle spirits. "We know that the whole of creation has been groaning in labor pains until now; and not only the creation, but we ourselves, who have the first fruits of the Spirit, groan inwardly while we wait for adoption, the redemption of our bodies" (Rom 8:22–23). How appropriate is the image of giving birth. The "life of the world to come" will include all the children born of mother earth: the "first fruits" is Jesus Christ, then those who belong to him (1 Cor 15:23), those who have "the first fruits of the Spirit," then the whole of creation so that finally "God may be all in all" (1 Cor 15:28). How are we to imagine this world to come? Surely not as some totally different, alien, and strange place with no connection to this earth! Rather it will be this world, the same world but now transformed by the creative power of God's Spirit into unity with the divine life, integral wholeness, and eternal life where death no longer has any power. This is what resurrection means (see Q. 68).

Q. 99. What about hell? Didn't Jesus say that evildoers will be thrown into the fire where there will be weeping and gnashing of teeth?

There is such a reference in Matthew's interpretation of the parable of the weeds of the field (Mt 13:36–43). Fire is a common biblical image of judgment (e.g. Mk 9:42–48 par.; Mt 3:10–12 par.; 7:19). The image comes from the fire of judgment burning in the valley of Hinnom (Jer 7:32; 19:6; Is 66:24), called in the NT "Gehenna." The OT also refers to "sheol," the shadow world of the dead. What the prophets, John the Baptist, and Jesus wish to convey by such imagery is the supreme importance of human decisions both for this life and for the life of the world to come. It is not a question of divine vengeance or arbitrary punishment. Rather, God has created us with a free will and respects the consequences of our choices, even when those choices involve a fatal turning away from God who is the only source of life.

The church has defined that hell exists, but it is useless to speculate on what it is like or where it is or whether anyone is in hell. Only God can make such judgments. However, to image hell we need to look no further than the hells we humans create through wars, ethnic hatreds, tortures, massacres, mass starvation, etc., etc. in this present world. The important thing about the church's doctrine of hell is not our capacity to imagine extreme physical torments that last forever, but the sense of unutterable loss that would come if we had rendered ourselves by our own choices eternally incapable of returning God's love. It is the intensity of God's love and our incapacity to respond that would forever torment us. What all this means is that God takes seriously what we do, that it makes a difference how we respond to the divine initiatives for the shape of the world to come. This is a God who dialogues, who desires that we become full and free human beings living forever within the divine circle of love, but who respects as sacred and inviolate our personal freedom.

Q. 100. What will Jesus' second coming be like?

It seems clear that the earliest Christian communities had a very strong expectation that Jesus would return as the Son of Man at any moment. Paul still seems to assume that Jesus will come during the lifetime of at least some of those to whom he is writing (1 Thes 4:13–5:11; 1 Cor 15:50–52). Yet, he will also come when least expected "like a thief in the night" (1 Thes 5:2; Mt 24:43–44 par.), so the most we can do is be ready. This is the main point of the synoptic apocalyptic discourses (Mk 13:1–37 par.). John manifests less of a sense of urgency since one who believes in Jesus Christ is already experiencing eternal life. Yet the book of Revelation, which comes from the Johannine community, ends with the yearning of every Christian: "Amen. Come, Lord Jesus!" (Rev 22:20).

The imagery of the Son of Man coming in clouds with great power and glory (Mk 13:26 par.) is intended to say that when the moment finally arrives no one will miss it or be able to evade it. It is the moment of final and decisive judgment. But what can be made of the fact that some two thousand years later we are still waiting for that moment? One can only speculate. But if we take seriously the fact that Jesus failed in his earthly mission and that as a consequence we continue to live under the sign of the cross, then perhaps God's creative intention for the transformation of the world that will include the destruction of "every ruler and every authority and power," of "all his enemies," the last of which is death (1 Cor 15:24–26), has simply needed more time and more space. Luke seems to sense that we are in for a longer time than originally imagined: "It is not for you to know the times or periods that the Father has set by his own authority" (Acts 1:7). We must still trust in divine providence (see Q. 64). Our hope remains that so beautifully expressed by Paul: "But our citizenship is in heaven, and it is from there that we are expecting a Savior, the Lord Jesus Christ. He will transform our humble bodies that they may be conformed to his glorious body, by the power that also enables him to make all things subject to himself" (Phil 3:20–21; tr. slightly altered from the NRSV). Amen. Come, Lord Jesus!

Q. 101. What do you think would happen if Jesus came back today?

I think he would ask the same question that he asked of his first disciples at Caesarea Philippi: "And you, who do you say that I am?" (Mk 8:29 par.). In the final analysis, it is not the many questions that we ask of Jesus that are important so much as the one vital question he asks of us. And how will we answer? How can we even begin to answer if we have not taken up our cross and followed him on the way? What Mark teaches us is that there can be no answer to the question of who Jesus is, nor of who we are as disciples, if we have not experienced how he died (Mk 15:39). Peter claimed vehemently that he would die with Jesus rather than deny him (Mk 14:27–31), but he did deny him. Yet it is the paradox and mystery of life that the ones who die are the ones who bring forth much fruit (Jn 12:24–26). What finally counts is doing the will of the Father by following Jesus on his way in the power of the Spirit of truth and of life.

GLOSSARY OF TERMS

Note: the parentheses refer to the place where the word first occurs.

APOCALYPTIC (Q. 33): derived from the Greek word for revelation (*apocalypsis*), it usually refers to a type of literature popular among both Jews and Christians from around 200 B.C.E. to 200 C.E. The last book of the NT, which is characteristic of this kind of literature, is called the Apocalypse or Revelation to John. Written in a time of persecution, such literature uses veiled or symbolic language and images to offer the community hope for final victory and encouragement to persevere. An extreme form of apocalyptic looks for "signs" to predict exactly when, where, and how the end of the world will take place, but biblical apocalyptic is more fundamentally protest literature that relies on God to realize the hopes of the community. For Christians, the final and definitive "apocalyptic event" has taken place in the resurrection of Jesus (see QQ. 68, 71, 98).

BIBLICAL CRITICISM (Introduction): the application of human reason (hence "criticism") to the texts of the OT and the NT. Such "reason" may be historical, philosophical, experiential, literary, etc. Methods are developed that correspond to the kinds of questions being asked. The development of "modern" biblical criticism is generally dated from the time of the enlightenment in the eighteenth century.

CHRISTOLOGY (Introduction): derived from the Greek words for Christ = Messiah (*christos*) and study (*logos*), it is the study of who

Jesus is and what Christians have said about him through the centuries. Such study, if it is to be true to the whole of Christian tradition, must include the historical Jesus, his death and resurrection, the developing understanding of his significance in the New Testament, in the creeds and councils, in the writings of theologians and the works of artists and mystics up to the present.

COUNCILS (Introduction): based on the model of Peter and Paul meeting with the leaders of the Jerusalem community in Acts 15 and on the growing need of local communities led by bishops to develop bonds with other local communities, consultations of bishops gathered together and including lay participation began in 175 and developed into "ecumenical" or worldwide councils under Constantine in 325. The ecumenical councils were called by the emperors, and their decrees, both doctrinal and disciplinary, had universal effect. The first seven from Nicea I (325) to Nicea II (787) were all concerned with major issues in Christology.

CREEDS (Introduction): officially recognized formulations of Christian faith. They can be as short as the NT formula: "Jesus is Lord!" or as long as the Nicene Creed recited every Sunday in church.

ESCHATOLOGY (Q. 70): derived from the Greek words for end (*eschaton*) and study (*logos*), it is the study of God's final intention for the whole of creation and especially for humans. The resurrection is sometimes called an "eschatological" or "apocalyptic" event by way of anticipation of the second coming of Christ and the final disposition of all things.

FATHERS OF THE CHURCH (Introduction): commonly referred to as the "patristic" period, this covers the writings of post-NT Christian authors from the time of St. Ignatius of Antioch (d. 110) to St. John of Damascus (d. 749). It is also the period of the first seven ecumenical councils (see above).

REVELATION (Q. 12): God's self-communication as mediated through nature, history, personal experience, etc. For Christians, God's self-communication comes primarily through Jesus who reveals the divine reality in a final and definitive way in the resurrection. All other claims to revelation must cohere with this once-for-all revelation (see QQ. 67–75).

SOTERIOLOGY (Q. 77): derived from the Greek words for salvation (*sōteria*) and study (*logos*), it is the study of God's intention for the salvation or liberation of creation. This is revealed primarily, though not exclusively, in Jesus' death and resurrection (see Q. 75). Christology and soteriology, i.e. who Jesus is and what he has accomplished, are inseparably connected.

SYNOPTIC GOSPELS (Introduction): the gospels of Matthew, Mark and Luke, so called because they can be placed in parallel columns to exhibit how much material they have in common. While the gospel of John has some material in common with the other three, it is markedly different in both outline and content.

BIBLIOGRAPHY

Note: Unless otherwise indicated, all direct quotations from the Bible are taken from *The New Oxford Annotated Bible with the Apocrypha,* eds. Bruce M. Metzger and Roland E. Murphy. New York: Oxford University Press, 1991 [NRSV].

Recommended for Further Reading:

Marcus J. Borg, *Jesus: A New Vision. Spirit, Culture, and the Life of Discipleship.* San Francisco: HarperCollins, 1987.

Raymond E. Brown, *Responses to 101 Questions on the Bible.* Mahwah: Paulist Press, 1990.

Michael L. Cook, *Guidelines for Contemporary Catholics: The Historical Jesus.* Chicago: The Thomas More Press, 1986.

Bernard J. Cooke, *God's Beloved: Jesus' Experience of the Transcendent.* Philadelphia: Trinity Press International, 1992.

James W. Douglass, *The Nonviolent Coming of God.* Maryknoll: Orbis Books, 1991.

Joseph A. Fitzmyer, *A Christological Catechism. New Testament Answers.* Ramsey: Paulist Press, 1982.

Andrew M. Greeley, *The Jesus Myth. New Insights into the Person and Message of Jesus.* New York: Doubleday Image Books, 1973.

Monika K. Hellwig, *Understanding Catholicism.* Ramsey: Paulist Press, 1981.

———, *Jesus, The Compassion of God.* Wilmington: Michael Glazier, 1983.

Elizabeth A. Johnson, *Consider Jesus. Waves of Renewal in Christology.* New York: Crossroad, 1990.

John P. Meier, *A Marginal Jew. Rethinking the Historical Jesus.* New York: Doubleday, 1991.

Juergen Moltmann, *The Way of Jesus Christ, Christology in Messianic Dimensions.* San Francisco: HarperCollins, 1990.

Albert Nolan, *Jesus Before Christianity.* Revised edition. Maryknoll: Orbis Books, 1992.

Jaroslav Pelikan, *Jesus Through the Centuries: His Place in the History of Culture.* New Haven: Yale University Press, 1985.

Sandra M. Schneiders, *Women and the Word. The Gender of God in the New Testament and the Spirituality of Women.* Mahwah: Paulist Press, 1986.

Gerard S. Sloyan, *Jesus in Focus. A Life in its Setting.* Mystic: Twenty-Third Publications, 1983.

———, *The Jesus Tradition. Images of Jesus in the West.* Mystic: Twenty-Third Publications, 1986.